pizza
and other savory pies

recipes by Brigit Binns

photographs by David Matheson

WELDON OWEN

Contents

Making Pizza at Home

Pizza is Italian in origin, but this humble flatbread with savory toppings has captured the attention of the entire planet. Pizza is enjoyed across the globe, and in every country where it's eaten it's tailored to the cultural palate. Take, for example, Mexico's ranchera pizza with beans and chorizo and India's seekh kebab pizza with kebabs of spiced ground meat. It's no wonder, really, that pizza's appeal is so far-reaching. Beneath the pepperoni, cheese, and tomato sauce that we have come to know and love in this country is a blank canvas—or dough—that's primed for all sorts of culinary renditions.

In Italy, however, pizza is made with a great deal of restraint and respect for tradition. Pizza Napoletana—or Neapolitan pizza—is widely regarded as the pizza par excellence, so much so that it's been given D.O.C. (Denominazione di Origine Controllata) status to protect its integrity. This means that only pizzas made according to certain strict standards can be called authentic Neapolitan pizza. There are only two primary types of traditional Neapolitan pizza: pizza marinara made with tomato sauce, garlic, and oregano, and pizza Margherita made with fresh tomatoes, fresh mozzarella, and basil.

In contrast to the Italian approach, in the United States, just as in other parts of the world, many liberties have been taken with the creation of pizza. Popular American pies include barbecued chicken pizza with smoky, tangy barbecue sauce; Hawaiian pizza topped with pineapple and Canadian bacon; and "The Works," a pizza blanketed with every imaginable topping. Then there are the regional pizzas: New York is known for its thin-crust pizza and Chicago for its deep-dish pies. Devotees of each will argue about which is the best.

Pizza is often considered convenience food because it's usually ordered out. Homemade pizza, however, is not about convenience—it's about enjoying the making and baking process, as well as the satisfaction that goes along with creating wholesome and delicious food. To help get you started with pizza-baking at home, this book contains all the recipes you need. It covers Italian classics like Pizza Margherita (page 36); American favorites like Classic Pepperoni Pizza (page 68); contemporary combinations like Salad-Topped Grilled Pizza (page 84); inspired pies like Jerk Chicken Pizza with Smoked Gouda and Red Onion (page 54); and pizza spin-offs, such as stromboli (page 97). You will also find recipes for different types of pizza doughs, recipes for pizza staples like tomato sauce, and, just as importantly, the inspiration to make and bake all sorts of fresh, flavorful pizzas at home.

Pizza equipment

DOUGH-MAKING EQUIPMENT

Pizza dough is easy to make and comes together quickly in a food processor or in a heavy-duty stand mixer with a dough hook attachment. The recipes in this book were developed using an 11-cup food processor. For more on making pizza dough, turn to page 12.

PIZZA STONE

Traditionally, pizzas are baked in coal- or wood-fired ovens with brick floors that produce crisp, brown crusts. To imitate the intense heat of a brick oven in a home oven, a pizza stone—a flat piece of unglazed stoneware—works beautifully. Pizza stones are available in rectangular and round shapes; a rectangular one will better accommodate a large or slightly misshapen pie. A pizza stone can be left in the oven for any baking or roasting that you need to do, but if you must remove it, first allow it to cool thoroughly. Caked-on bits of food can be scrubbed off with a scouring pad and warm water; do not use sudsy water, as the soap will seep into pores of the stone. Unglazed terracotta tiles or baking tiles are good alternatives to a pizza stone—they need to be pieced together to line the oven rack. If you don't have a pizza stone or baking tiles, you can use a large heavy-duty baking sheet (solid, heavy construction ensures that the pan will not warp), preheating it just as you would a stone.

PIZZA PEEL

A pizza peel, sometimes called a baker's peel, is a wide paddle made of wood or metal, attached to a long handle. It's used to slide freeform pizzas and breads onto and off of a hot pizza stone because it's too treacherous to handle the heavy pizza stone itself. Pizzas can be formed directly on the peel so that they do not need to be transferred once they are topped. Though it takes a few tries to learn to use a pizza peel skillfully (it requires a quick, decisive motion to get the items off of and onto the peel), it's a useful piece of equipment for any avid pizza baker. A baking sheet can stand in for a pizza peel, but it must be rimless so that a pizza can easily slide off and on.

KNIVES AND CUTTERS

A chef's knife is an indispensible kitchen tool for any cook, pizza-bakers included. It's not only used for preparing the ingredients that go on top of a pizza, it's also useful for cutting the baked pizza for serving. To slice your pizza, use the largest chef's knife you own, preferably one with an 8- to 10-inch blade. Place the tip of the knife at the center of the pie with the knife handle angled upward. Press down on the back of the upper part of the blade with your other hand to steady the blade and make sure that the tip of the knife cuts through the bottom crust. Lower the knife handle to cut through the pie; before removing the knife, make sure that you have cut all the way through the bottom crust. Repeat to cut the rest of the pizza. For some shape variety, you can cut oval or rectangular pizzas into strips, rectangles, or squares.

For slicing baked pizzas, a pizza wheel is not a necessity, but it's a handy tool to have, especially if you make pizza often. With one quick movement, a pizza wheel allows you to cut cleanly through the toppings and crust. A pizza wheel is also a boon for bakers who trim rolled doughs and cut unbaked pastry into strips and rounds. When shopping, look for a solidly built pizza wheel with a comfortable, secure grip and a large, sturdy blade.

The secret to problem-free pizza

Before a pizza is formed on the pizza peel, the peel is usually dusted with flour, semolina, or sometimes cornmeal to ensure that the dough will slide off easily into the oven. Though this method works well in commercial kitchens, it is less sensible in home kitchens, as the flour is prone to burning in the high heat of the oven. Parchment paper is the solution to this problem. Shaping and baking the pizza on a large sheet of parchment paper eliminates the need to use flour—the parchment acts as a liner that allows the pizza to slide smoothly from pizza peel to pizza stone and vice versa. Parchment paper is heat-resistant, so it will not burn, and is thin enough that it will not interfere with the formation of the crust. Unbleached parchment paper is brown in color; regular parchment is bright white. They work equally well, but try to purchase parchment paper that is at least 14 inches wide so that it is large enough accommodate a full-sized pizza. Do not substitute waxed paper for parchment because it cannot withstand high oven temperatures.

Pizza ingredients

DOUGH INGREDIENTS

Just a handful of basic ingredients is all that is needed to make pizza dough at home. All-purpose flour, a kitchen staple, is the foundation for almost all of the pizza doughs in this book. All-purpose flour is often bleached to produce a pure white color, but this bleaching process also adversely affects flavor. Unbleached all-purpose flour has a fuller, nuttier, more complex flavor than bleached all-purpose flour. The dough recipes in this book that call for all-purpose flour were developed using the unbleached variety. Bread flour, whole-wheat flour, and semolina flour are the other types of flour that are used to make pizza doughs; for more information about these flours, consult the glossary, which starts on page 106.

Yeast is a microorganism that is used to naturally leaven breads—that is, get them to rise so that they bake up with airy, open structures. With the exception of the Semolina Pizza Dough (page 23), which uses active dry yeast, the dough recipes in this book were developed using quick-rise yeast; both types are commonly available in grocery stores. They are not interchangeable, so be sure to use the exact type of yeast called for.

Salt heightens and improves the flavor of any food to which it is added, including pizza dough. For pizza dough, it's best to use fine- to medium-grained salt—such as table salt and kosher salt—so that the granules will be easily and evenly distributed throughout.

Just a small measure of olive oil gives pizza dough richness as well as some suppleness. It's not necessary to use your finest extra-virgin olive oil to make pizza dough, but do try to use an olive oil with good flavor.

TOPPING INGREDIENTS

It goes without saying: To create the most flavorful pizzas, use the best-quality and freshest ingredients that you can find. Salt and pepper—the most basic of seasonings—go a long way in adding flavor. A few recipes in this book call specifically for coarse sea salt as a topping because it adds texture and bursts of saltiness. Freshly ground black peppercorns from a pepper mill offer the fullest, spiciest black-pepper flavor.

Look for authentic cheeses at cheesemongers or specialty food stores that sell their stock quickly so that you're assured the freshest cheese. In the case of Parmigiano-Reggiano, a good grating and eating cheese to keep on hand, it's best to purchase only as much as you plan to use in a couple of weeks so that it doesn't dry out or turn moldy. Grate or shred cheese yourself at home instead of buying the pre-grated or pre-shredded varieties.

Try to purchase produce from local growers or farmers' markets. Tomatoes should be plump, vibrant in color, and blemish free. Heads of garlic should be tight, firm, and without green shoots sprouting from the tops of the cloves. Other produce, such as eggplant, should be firm and blemish free. Fresh herbs should be bright green and possess a heady fragrance. Some recipes in this book call for dried herbs because they offer a unique flavor profile that is particularly suited to pizza. Make sure that the dried herbs from your pantry are flavorful and fragrant.

Some of the pizza recipes call for drizzling the baked pizza with olive oil just before serving to add luster and flavor. This is the time to use your fine extra-virgin olive oil with rich, fruity flavor.

Making the dough

WORKING WITH YEAST

Most of the dough recipes in this book call for quick-rise yeast, which can be added directly to the other dough ingredients. Active dry yeast, however, must be "proofed" before it can be used.

To proof active dry yeast, sprinkle it over warm water (about 110°F) in a bowl or measuring cup; adding a little bit of sugar helps to activate the yeast more quickly. Upon standing for 5–10 minutes, the yeast should become foamy. (UPPER LEFT) If it doesn't become foamy, the yeast is most likely dead and unusable. It's best to start over with new active dry yeast.

MAKING THE DOUGH

A food processor makes quick work of making pizza dough—with just a few quick pulses and less than a minute of processing, the dough is formed. The doughs in this book were developed using an 11-cup food processor. (A smaller machine cannot handle the dough quantity.) In a food processor, the dry ingredients are pulsed together and the liquids are added while the machine is running. The dough will come together in a rough mass. Let it rest for 5–10 minutes and then process it again for about 30 seconds more to fully develop the protein and make the dough resilient. (UPPER RIGHT)

You can also make pizza dough in a standing mixer: Fit the mixer with the dough hook attachment and follow the basic food processor procedure; however, the mixing times for a standing mixer will be significantly longer. The final knead, after the 5–10 minute rest, should result in a smooth, elastic dough and can take up to 10 minutes.

No matter how you make the dough, once it is kneaded, it should be soft and smooth and should feel moist and slightly tacky to the touch, but not at all wet or sticky.

LETTING THE DOUGH RISE

During rising, the dough develops the complex flavors and texture that are characteristic of yeasted breads. Place the dough in a lightly oiled bowl and then turn the dough over so that the top is lightly coated with oil. Cover the bowl with plastic wrap or a clean kitchen towel. The film of oil will prevent the surface of the dough from drying out as it rises. A draft-free spot is ideal for allowing the dough to rise; warmth will cause it to rise quickly, and cool temperatures will slow it down. When the dough is puffy and has doubled in volume, which takes about 1½ hours in a warm spot, it is ready to use. (BOTTOM LEFT)

DIVIDING THE DOUGH

Turn the risen dough out onto a lightly floured work surface and gently punch it down to knock out the air. Work the dough into a cylinder of even thickness. (This shape is easy to divide evenly.) Using a chef's knife, cut the cylinder in half, or as directed in the recipe. Shape each piece of dough into a ball by cupping your hands around its sides and moving the dough along the work surface in a circular motion; the dough's tackiness against the surface should help pull it into a compact ball (BOTTOM RIGHT) that will be easy to roll or stretch out into an even round. If you are using only one piece of dough, as most of the recipes in this book specify, place the extra dough ball in a gallon-size zipper-lock plastic bag, press out the air, and seal it well. Freeze the dough for up to 2 months; let it thaw at room temperature for 2–3 hours before use.

Shaping and topping your pizza

SHAPING THE DOUGH ROUND

Freeform pizzas—those that are not baked in a pan—can be shaped directly on a large piece of parchment paper so that they can be easily transferred to the pizza stone. For certain pies like the super-thin-crusted Pizza Margherita (page 36), a rolling pin is handy to form the dough into an ultra-thin round. For most other pizzas, however, your hands are all you need. Hand-formed pizzas tend to have more character—they have slightly irregular shapes and are more likely to bake up with bubbles because not all the air is pressed out of the dough as it is when the dough is rolled with a rolling pin.

Set the dough ball on a large sheet of parchment paper. Coat your fingers with olive oil to prevent them from sticking to the dough. Then, using your palms and fingers, push, pat, and press the dough outward from the center, leaving the edge slightly thicker. (UPPER LEFT)

Keep in mind that the thinner you make your dough round, the crisper it will bake up. If, while you shape the dough, it becomes elastic and shrinks back, cover it with a kitchen towel and allow it to rest for about 15 minutes before proceeding. Resting gives the gluten—the protein in the flour that was developed during kneading—a chance to relax so that the dough is more workable. Pizza dough can be shaped as a circle, an oval, or even a rectangle. If, in the end, your pie ends up misshapen, don't worry—such imperfections make a pizza look rustic and handcrafted.

ALLOWING THE DOUGH ROUND TO RISE

After shaping the dough, cover it with a clean kitchen towel and let it rise on the work surface for about 15 minutes. This brief second rise before the dough is topped allows it to develop just a little bit of volume so that it doesn't bake up heavy and dense. (UPPER RIGHT)

OILING AND SEASONING THE DOUGH ROUND

After the second rise and before topping the dough, brush the edges or the entire round with olive oil. This light coating of oil helps the edges bake up golden brown and crisp. It is not necessary to use extra-virgin olive oil here—regular olive oil does a fine job. (BOTTOM LEFT)

Before being topped, the dough round is often seasoned with salt and pepper. This helps bring the flavors of the crust and toppings together and heightens the flavor of each bite. (BOTTOM RIGHT)

TOPPING THE DOUGH ROUND

Authentic Neapolitan pizzas are topped with a light hand, allowing the flavorful crust to share the spotlight with the toppings. The pizzas in this book follow this approach. Layer the toppings on the dough round, usually beginning with the sauce. Leave a 1/2-inch border free so that the pizza bakes up with a crisp, brown edge. If you're opting to use your own selection of toppings, make sure that they are not very heavy or wet, which will cause the crust to bake up soggy and doughy. The dough recipes in the Pizza Basics chapter make enough dough to form two regular pies, but most of the pizza recipes make enough topping for only pie. Therefore, if you're making two pizzas with the same toppings, remember to double the amount of ingredients. Or, mix it up by choosing two recipes and using different toppings on each pizza. After all, making customized pies that are tailored to your own palate is one of the great things about baking pizza at home.

Baking pizza

Neapolitan and commercial pizza ovens reach very high temperatures, usually in excess of 700°F. With such high heat, thin-crust pizzas bake in just a couple of minutes. Home ovens don't generate this kind of intense heat, which is why it is important to use a pizza stone. A pizza stone absorbs and retains heat so that the oven temperature does not drop drastically each time the oven door is opened. For thicker pizzas like deep-dish pizza (page 93), and for filled variations on pizza, such as calzone (page 94) and stromboli (page 97), lower oven temperatures ensure that the interiors bake through without the exteriors scorching.

To get your pizza into the oven, hold the peel in one hand and rest the edge on the pizza stone. Quickly slide the pizza-topped parchment paper onto the pizza stone, using your other hand to help, if needed. Bake the pizza until the crust is golden and crisp and the cheese is bubbling. Then, to remove the pizza from the oven, slip the pizza peel between the parchment and the pizza stone–if necessary, carefully grab a section of the parchment and pull the parchment with the pizza onto the peel.

Grilling pizza

Cooking pizza on the grill infuses the pie with hints of smokiness and is a great alternative to heating up the kitchen in the throes of summer. Because pizza dough readily burns if cooked directly over the flames, the grill must be set up so that the pizza can be cooked over indirect heat. If necessary, shape your pizzas into ovals or a shape that will fit onto the area that will be the cool side of the grill. Pizzas must grilled one at a time and in relatively

rapid succession, so if you're cooking multiples, be sure you're organized and have all your tools and ingredients ready before you put the first one on the grill grate.

To prepare a charcoal grill for grilling pizza, pour one large chimney starter's worth of ignited coals into the grill bottom, and then use long-handled tongs to arrange the coals on either side of the grill, dividing them evenly and leaving the center of the grill coal-free. Cover the grill and allow the grill grate to heat for 5–10 minutes. Once the grill is heated, lift the cover and scrape the grill grate with a stiff wire brush to remove any grease or food residue.

To prepare a gas grill, turn all the burners to high and close the lid. Allow the grill to heat for 10–15 minutes. If you own a grill thermometer, check to make sure that the internal temperature of the grill reaches 500°F. Once the grill is heated, lift the cover and scrape the grill grate clean with a stiff wire brush to remove any food residue. Turn off one or more of the burners so that there is flame beneath only half of the cooking area.

To cook pizza on a charcoal or gas grill, have all your ingredients ready before you begin; this process goes quickly! Using a pair of long-handled tongs, lightly dip a wad of paper towels into vegetable oil and then wipe the heat-free zone of the grill grate with the oil-soaked towels. This will help prevent the pizza dough from sticking to the grate. Unlike an oven-baked pizza, a grilled pizza is not topped before baking, because the dough round must be flipped during cooking. Start by placing the dough round on the cool area of the grill. Once the first side is browned, use a long-handled spatula to flip the dough, quickly top it, and cook it, covered, until the cheese is melted and the bottom is browned.

Serving your pizza with style

In general, pizza is best hot out of the oven, with only a minute or two of rest to allow the toppings to cool down slightly so that they will not slide off when the pieces are pulled apart. Delicate herbs and a last-minute drizzle of extra-virgin olive oil are put on the pizza right at the end, just before it is cut, to add fresh color and flavor. If you're making multiple pizzas but have only one pizza stone, top the second pizza while the first one bakes. When the first one is done, it's best to serve it without delay, though it can wait ten or so minutes until the second one is ready.

To serve a full-sized round pizza as an appetizer, cut it into slender wedges; as a main course, slice it into sixths or eighths. Cut mini pizzas in half or quarters for serving. Halve oval and rectangular pizzas along their length and then cut them into narrow or wide strips, or rectangles or squares. For a casual gathering or meal, serve your pizza directly from the cutting board; at a party or more formal affair, plate it on a flat, wide platter. Bring it to the table, and invite everyone to enjoy. Mangia!

Pizza Basics

Thin-Crust Pizza Dough

3⅓ cups all-purpose flour, plus extra for dusting

¼ cup whole-wheat flour

1 package (2½ tsp) quick-rise yeast

1 tbsp sugar

1 tbsp salt

1¼ cups warm water (110°F), plus extra as needed

2 tbsp olive oil, plus extra as needed

In a food processor, combine the all-purpose flour, whole-wheat flour, yeast, sugar, and salt. Pulse to mix the ingredients. With the motor running, add the water and olive oil in a steady stream, and then pulse until the dough comes together in a rough mass, about 12 seconds. If the dough does not form into a ball, sprinkle with 1–2 teaspoons of water and pulse again until a rough mass forms. Let the dough rest for 5–10 minutes. Process again for 25–30 seconds, steadying the top of the food processor with one hand. The dough should be tacky to the touch but not sticky. Transfer the dough to a lightly floured work surface and form it into a smooth ball. Place the dough in a large oiled bowl, turn to coat with oil, and cover with plastic wrap. Let the dough rise in a warm place until doubled in bulk and spongy (see page 12), about 1½ hours.

Turn the dough out onto a lightly floured work surface, punch it down, and shape into a smooth cylinder. Divide the dough into 2 equal pieces. Shape each piece into a smooth ball, dusting with flour only if the dough becomes sticky. Cover both balls of dough with a clean kitchen towel and let rest for 10 minutes before proceeding with your chosen pizza recipe. If you are using only one ball of dough, place the second ball in a gallon-size zipper-lock bag and freeze for up to 2 months. (When ready to use, thaw the frozen dough for 3–4 hours at room temperature.)

MAKES 2 BALLS OF DOUGH

Versatile thin-crust pizza dough can be used to make many different types of pizza, including calzone and stromboli. When shaping a pizza, keep in mind that the thinner the dough is stretched, the crisper the crust will be.

Deep-Dish Pizza Dough

3¾ cups bread flour, plus extra for dusting

⅔ cup medium-ground cornmeal

1½ tbsp sugar

1 tbsp kosher salt

1 package (2½ tsp) quick-rise yeast

1½ cups warm water (110°F), plus extra as needed

5 tbsp olive oil, plus extra as needed

In a food processor, combine the flour, cornmeal, sugar, salt, and yeast. Pulse to mix the ingredients. With the motor running, add the water and olive oil in a steady stream, then pulse until the dough comes together in a rough mass, about 12 seconds. If the dough does not form into a ball, sprinkle with 1–2 teaspoons of water and pulse again until a rough mass forms. Let rest for 5–10 minutes. Process again for 25–30 seconds, steadying the top of the food processor with one hand. The dough should be tacky to the touch but not sticky. Transfer the dough to a lightly floured work surface and form it into a smooth ball. Place the dough in a large oiled bowl, turn to coat with oil, and cover with plastic wrap. Let the dough rise in a warm place until doubled in bulk and spongy (see page 12), about 2 hours.

Turn the dough out onto a lightly floured work surface, punch it down, and shape into a smooth cylinder. Divide the dough into 2 equal pieces. Shape each piece into a smooth ball, dusting with flour only if the dough becomes sticky. Cover both balls of dough with a clean kitchen towel and let rest for 10 minutes before proceeding with the pizza recipe. If you are using only one ball of dough, place the second ball in a gallon-size zipper-lock bag and freeze for up to 2 months. (When ready to use, thaw the frozen dough for 3–4 hours at room temperature.)

MAKES 2 BALLS OF DOUGH

Chicago takes credit as the undisputed birthplace of all-American deep-dish pizza. The crust of a deep-dish pizza should be rich and tender, with a soft, open crumb, and its sides should be tall, thick, and sturdy enough to encase a wealth of flavorful filling.

Semolina Pizza Dough

In a measuring pitcher, stir together the warm water and the sugar and sprinkle with the yeast. Let the mixture stand until it starts to foam, about 5 minutes. Add the 1 cup room-temperature water and the olive oil.

In a food processor, combine the semolina flour, all-purpose flour, and salt. With the motor running, add the yeast-water mixture in a steady stream, and then pulse until the dough comes together in a rough mass, about 12 seconds. If the dough does not form into a ball, sprinkle with 1–2 teaspoons of water and pulse again until a rough mass forms. Let rest for 5–10 minutes. Process again for 25–30 seconds, steadying the top of the food processor with one hand. The dough should be tacky to the touch but not sticky. Transfer the dough to a lightly floured work surface and form it into a smooth ball. Place the dough in a large oiled bowl, turn to coat with oil, and cover with plastic wrap. Let the dough rise in a warm place until doubled in bulk and spongy (see page 12), about 1½ hours.

Turn the dough out onto a lightly floured work surface, punch it down, and shape into a smooth cylinder. Divide the dough into 2 equal pieces. Shape each piece into a smooth ball, dusting with flour only if the dough becomes sticky. Cover both balls of dough with a clean kitchen towel and let rest for 10 minutes before proceeding with your chosen pizza recipe. If you are using only one ball of dough, place the second ball in a gallon-size zipper-lock bag and freeze for up to 2 months. (When ready to use, thaw the frozen dough for 3–4 hours at room temperature.)

MAKES 2 BALLS OF DOUGH

¼ cup warm water (120°F)

1 tsp sugar

1 package (2½ tsp) active dry yeast

1 cup room-temperature water, plus extra as needed

1 tbsp olive oil, plus extra as needed

2 cups plus 2 tbsp fine semolina flour

1 cup plus 7 tbsp all-purpose flour, plus extra for dusting

1 tbsp salt

Semolina is a protein-rich flour that makes this dough resilient and gives the baked crust a hearty chew and tooth-sinking texture. Semolina dough is ideal for Egg, Sausage & Cheese Breakfast Pizzas (page 90) and Pizza Rustica (page 98).

Whole-Wheat Pizza Dough

In a food processor, combine the all-purpose flour, whole-wheat flour, yeast, salt, and sugar. Pulse to mix the ingredients. With the motor running, add the water and olive oil in a steady stream, and then pulse until the dough comes together in a rough mass, about 12 seconds. If the dough does not form into a ball, sprinkle with 1–2 teaspoons of water and pulse again until a rough mass forms. Let rest for 5–10 minutes. Process again for 25–30 seconds, steadying the top of the food processor with one hand. The dough should be tacky to the touch but not sticky. Transfer the dough to a lightly floured work surface and form it into a smooth ball. Place the dough in a large oiled bowl, turn to coat with oil, and cover with plastic wrap. Let the dough rise in a warm place until doubled in bulk and spongy (see page 12), about 1½ hours.

Turn the dough out onto a lightly floured work surface, punch it down, and knead into a smooth cylinder. Divide the dough into 2 equal pieces. Shape each piece into a smooth ball, dusting with flour only if the dough becomes sticky. Cover both balls of dough with a clean kitchen towel and let rest for 10 minutes before proceeding with your chosen pizza recipe. If you are using only one ball of dough, place the second ball in a gallon-size zipper-lock bag and freeze for up to 2 months. (When ready to use, thaw the frozen dough for 3–4 hours at room temperature.)

MAKES 2 BALLS OF DOUGH

2¼ cups all-purpose flour, plus extra for dusting

1⅓ cups whole-wheat flour

1 package (2½ tsp) quick-rise yeast

2 tsp salt

1 tsp sugar

1¼ cups warm water (110°F), plus extra as needed

2 tbsp olive oil, plus extra as needed

The trick to delicious whole-wheat pizza dough is adding enough whole-wheat flour to give the crust rich, nutty flavor, but not so much that it bakes up heavy and dense. This recipe strikes a perfect balance and can be used to make almost any type of pizza.

Simple Tomato Sauce

¼ cup olive oil

5 cloves garlic, minced

1 can (15 oz) crushed tomatoes

1 tsp dried basil

¾ tsp dried oregano

¼ tsp dried thyme

¼ tsp freshly ground pepper

1½–2 tbsp red wine vinegar

Salt

In a small frying pan over medium heat, warm the olive oil. Add the garlic and cook, stirring frequently, until fragrant, 1–2 minutes. Be careful not to let it scorch or the garlic will taste bitter.

In a bowl, stir together the garlic-oil mixture, tomatoes, dried basil, dried oregano, dried thyme, pepper, ⅓ cup of water, and 1½ tablespoons of the vinegar. Season to taste with salt and additional vinegar. Use right away or refrigerate in an airtight container for up to 1 week.

MAKES ABOUT 2¾ CUPS

Canned tomatoes vary in salt content, so to start, season the sauce with just a pinch of salt and then gradually add more to taste. When seasoning with the red wine vinegar, add just enough to make the flavor really sparkle; the sauce shouldn't taste tangy.

Black Olive Tapenade

1²/₃ cups brine-cured black olives

3 anchovy fillets

3 tbsp capers, rinsed and drained

3 cloves garlic, finely chopped

1½ tbsp brandy

3 tbsp fresh lemon juice

½ tsp freshly ground white pepper

¼ cup extra-virgin olive oil

1½ tbsp coarsely chopped fresh flat-leaf parsley leaves

On a cutting board, spread the olives in a single layer. Lay the flat side of the blade of a chef's knife on top of the olives and, applying pressure with your hand, gently crush the olives so that the flesh splits. Using your fingers, remove and discard the olive pits.

Rinse the anchovy fillets and pat them dry with paper towels.

In a food processor, combine the olives, anchovies, capers, garlic, brandy, lemon juice, and white pepper. Pulse once or twice to chop roughly, and then add the olive oil and pulse briefly until combined, scraping down the sides of the bowl once or twice. The texture should be chunky. Transfer the mixture to a bowl and stir in the parsley. Use right away or refrigerate in an airtight container for up to 2 days.

MAKES ABOUT 1³/₄ CUPS

This rustic, chunky spread is full of the bold flavors of the Mediterranean. To be true to tapenade's French Provençal roots, make it using the tiny, meaty-flavored, and relatively mild-tasting Niçoise olives.

Sun-Dried Tomato Pesto

If you are using dry-packed sun-dried tomatoes, place them in a heatproof bowl and cover them with hot water. Let them soak until soft and pliable, about 20 minutes. Drain the sun-dried tomatoes and squeeze them to remove excess moisture. (If you are using oil-packed sun-dried tomatoes, you can skip this step.)

In a food processor, combine the sun-dried tomatoes, thyme leaves, and 1–2 tablespoons olive oil. Process to a smooth paste, adding more olive oil, as needed, until a thick, spreadable mixture forms, about 20 seconds, scraping down the sides of the bowl once or twice. Use right away or refrigerate in an airtight container for up to 1 week.

MAKES ABOUT ½ CUP

½ cup dry-packed or oil-packed sun-dried tomatoes

½ tsp fresh thyme leaves

Extra-virgin olive oil, as needed

Sun-dried tomatoes contain the concentrated sweet-tart essence of red, ripe tomatoes. If you're opting to use dry-packed sun-dried tomatoes, look for ones that feel moist, plump, and pliant, a good indicator that the tomatoes are fresh.

Basil Pesto

To toast the pine nuts, in a small dry frying pan, warm the pine nuts over medium heat, shaking the pan occasionally, until fragrant and lightly browned, 2–3 minutes. Transfer the nuts to a plate and let cool to room temperature.

Fill a saucepan with water, bring to a boil over high heat, and season lightly with table salt. Add the basil and let cook for 10 seconds, remove with a slotted spoon, and plunge into a bowl of ice water. Let stand for 1 minute to halt the cooking. Remove the basil from the ice bath and squeeze the leaves dry with your hands to remove as much excess moisture as possible.

In a food processor, combine the toasted pine nuts, basil, garlic, olive oil, and $1/8$ teaspoon sea salt. Process for about 30 seconds, scraping down the sides of the bowl once or twice. Add the cheese and process until combined, about 5 seconds more. Season to taste with additional sea salt. Use right away or refrigerate in an airtight container for up to 2 days.

MAKES 1 CUP

2 tbsp pine nuts

2½ cups fresh basil leaves

Table salt

5 garlic cloves, coarsely chopped

¾ cup extra-virgin olive oil

Fine sea salt

2 tbsp grated Parmigiano-Reggiano

Salty, savory Black Olive Tapenade (top left, page 28); sweet, intense Sun-Dried Tomato Pesto (center, page 29); and herbal, garlicky Basil Pesto (bottom) are all easy-to-make base toppings that add rich and robust flavors to your pizzas.

Savory Caramelized Onions

2 tbsp olive oil

2 small yellow onions, halved lengthwise and thinly sliced

1 clove garlic, minced

Salt and freshly ground pepper

In a cast-iron or nonstick frying pan over medium-low heat, warm the oil. Add the onions and 1 tablespoon of water, cover, and cook, stirring occasionally, until softened, about 20 minutes. Uncover and cook, stirring more frequently, until much of the liquid has evaporated and the onions are slightly golden, 5–10 minutes more. Be careful not to let them scorch.

Stir in the garlic and cook until fragrant and combined, about 1 minute. Season to taste with salt and pepper. Use right away or refrigerate in an airtight container for up to 1 day.

MAKES ABOUT 1¼ CUPS

These caramelized onions get a decidedly savory edge from the addition of a clove of garlic stirred in at the end of cooking. You can use sweet onions here, such as Vidalia onions, but they will caramelize much more quickly because they contain more sugar.

Marinated Roasted Peppers

If you are using a fresh red bell pepper, roast the pepper over a gas flame, turning occasionally with tongs, until the skin is blistered and blackened, but not ashy, all over, 4–6 minutes. Alternatively, broil the pepper under a preheated broiler about 2 inches from the heat, turning every 5 minutes, until the skin is blistered and blackened, but not ashy, all over, 15–20 minutes. Transfer the pepper to a bowl and cover tightly with plastic wrap. Let stand for 10–15 minutes. Slide the skin off with your fingers or a clean kitchen towel. Remove and discard the stem. (If you are using a jarred bell pepper, you can skip this step.)

Place the bell pepper on a cutting board and cut it so that it lies flat. Remove and discard the seeds and ribs, and then cut the pepper into thin strips.

In a bowl, stir together the olive oil, garlic, and oregano. Add the pepper strips and toss to coat. Season to taste with salt and pepper. Let the peppers marinate for at least 30 minutes or for up to 1 hour at room temperature. Use right away or refrigerate in an airtight container for up to 4 days.

MAKES ABOUT 1 CUP

1 large red bell pepper or 1 large jarred fire-roasted red bell pepper

1 tbsp olive oil

1 large clove garlic, minced

$1/4$ tsp dried oregano

Salt and freshly ground pepper

Plain roasted bell peppers are a good pizza topping, but marinating in garlic and herbs really punches up their flavor and makes them outstanding. If you're using jarred roasted peppers, look for whole ones; if they're unavailable, use 1 cup of pepper pieces.

Vegetable & Cheese Pizzas

Pizza Margherita

All-purpose flour

1 ball Thin-Crust Pizza Dough (page 20), at room temperature

Olive oil for shaping and brushing

Salt and freshly ground pepper

5 plum tomatoes or 3 large vine-ripened tomatoes, sliced ¼ inch thick

5 oz *mozzarella di bufala*, sliced and then torn into bite-sized pieces

6–8 large fresh basil leaves, torn into ¾-inch pieces

Extra-virgin olive oil for drizzling

This classic pizza features the colors of the Italian flag. It was created in the late nineteenth century and named for Italy's Queen Margherita.

Place a pizza stone on a rack in the lower third of the oven and preheat to 450°F. Let the pizza stone heat for 45–60 minutes.

On a lightly floured work surface, divide the dough in half and shape each half into a ball. Cover one of the balls with a clean kitchen towel and set aside. Place a large sheet of parchment paper on a pizza peel or large rimless baking sheet and place the first ball of dough in the center. Dust the top of the dough with flour and, using a rolling pin, roll out to a 9-inch round of even thickness. Cover the dough round with a clean kitchen towel and let rise for 15 minutes.

Coat your fingers with olive oil and press the dough outward from the center into a 14-inch round of even thickness (see page 15). Use your knuckles and the side of your palm in a rolling motion to gently coax the dough out from the center. If the dough springs back, cover it with a clean kitchen towel and let it rest for a few minutes, then continue. Patience is the key here, as the thinner the dough is, the crisper the crust will be. The resulting round should be very thin, about ¹⁄₁₆ inch.

Brush the dough with a light coating of olive oil and season lightly with salt and pepper. Arrange one-half of the sliced tomatoes over the dough so that they are almost touching one another, leaving a ½-inch border uncovered. Top with one-half of the mozzarella. Season lightly again with salt and pepper. Carefully slide the pizza-topped parchment paper from the peel or baking sheet onto the hot pizza stone. Bake until the crust is golden brown and the cheese is bubbling, 9–12 minutes. Meanwhile, shape and top the second pizza as above.

Using the pizza peel or rimless baking sheet, remove the pizza from the oven and transfer it to a cutting board. Let the pizza stand for 2 minutes. Meanwhile, bake the second pizza as above. Scatter the first pizza with one-half of the basil, drizzle with the extra-virgin olive oil, and slice. Serve the first pizza right away or wait until the second pizza is baked, topped with the remaining basil, and drizzled with extra-virgin olive oil and serve both pizzas together.

MAKES TWO 14-INCH THIN-CRUST PIZZAS; SERVES 3–4

Pizza with Pesto, Cherry Tomatoes & Mozzarella

Place a pizza stone on a rack in the lower third of the oven and preheat to 450°F. Let the pizza stone heat for 45–60 minutes.

Place a large sheet of parchment paper on a pizza peel or large rimless baking sheet and place the ball of dough in the center. Coat your fingers with olive oil and press the dough from the center outward into a 12-inch round with a slightly raised edge (see page 15). If the dough springs back, cover it with a clean kitchen towel and let it rest for a few minutes, then continue. Patience is the key here, as the thinner the dough is, the crisper the crust will be. Cover the dough round with a clean kitchen towel and let rise for 15 minutes.

Brush the raised edge of the dough with a light coating of olive oil. Spread the dough evenly with the pesto, leaving a $1/2$-inch border uncovered. Scatter the tomatoes over the pesto, top with the mozzarella, and season generously with salt and pepper. Carefully slide the pizza-topped parchment paper from the peel or baking sheet onto the hot pizza stone. Bake until the crust is golden brown and the cheese is bubbling, 9–12 minutes.

Using the pizza peel or rimless baking sheet, remove the pizza from the oven and transfer it to a cutting board. Let stand for 1 minute, and then slice and serve.

MAKES ONE 12-INCH PIZZA; SERVES 2–4

1 ball Thin-Crust Pizza Dough (page 20) or Whole-Wheat Pizza Dough (page 25), at room temperature

Olive oil for shaping and brushing

$1/2$ cup Basil Pesto (page 31)

6 oz cherry tomatoes, halved if large, left whole if small

$1/4$ lb *mozzarella di bufala*, sliced and then torn into bite-sized pieces

Salt and freshly ground pepper

This pizza is another take on the classic trio of Italian flavors: sweet tomatoes, fragrant basil, and creamy mozzarella cheese. Using cherry tomatoes of different colors makes a pizza that's a feast for the eyes as well as the taste buds.

Pizzette with Garlic, Mushrooms & Goat Cheese

32 garlic cloves, peeled

1 cup olive oil

2 tbsp olive oil, plus extra for shaping and brushing

2 shallots, minced

8 oz mixed wild and cultivated mushrooms, trimmed of woody stems, brushed clean, and thickly sliced

Coarse salt or kosher salt

Freshly ground pepper

All-purpose flour

1 ball Thin-Crust Pizza Dough (page 20) or Whole-Wheat Pizza Dough (page 25), at room temperature

4 oz fresh goat cheese, crumbled

Extra-virgin olive oil for drizzling

7 large fresh basil leaves, torn into small pieces

To make the caramelized garlic, in a small saucepan over medium-low heat, cover the garlic cloves with the olive oil. Cook until the cloves are just pale golden brown, about 10 minutes. Set aside and let cool.

Place a pizza stone on a rack in the lower third of the oven and preheat to 450°F. Let the pizza stone heat for 45–60 minutes. Meanwhile, in a large frying pan over medium-low heat, warm the 2 tablespoons olive oil. Add the shallots and cook, stirring frequently, until softened, about 3 minutes. Add the mushrooms and season generously with salt and pepper. Cook, stirring occasionally, until the mushrooms are softened and lightly golden, about 10 minutes.

On a lightly floured work surface, divide the dough into 16 equal balls. Coat your fingers with olive oil and press each ball into a flat 2½-inch round. If the dough springs back, cover with a clean kitchen towel and let it rest for a few minutes, then continue. Patience is the key here, as the thinner the rounds are, the crisper the crusts will be. Cover the rounds with a kitchen towel and let rise for 10 minutes.

Place a large sheet of parchment paper on each of 2 large rimless baking sheets. Space 8 dough rounds evenly on each sheet of parchment paper. Dimple the center the dough rounds with your fingertips, brush the edges with a light coating of olive oil, and lightly season the dough rounds with salt and pepper. Spoon 2 garlic cloves onto each round, then divide the mushrooms and cheese evenly among the rounds. Bake one sheet at a time on the pizza stone until the crusts are golden brown, 8–10 minutes.

Remove the pizzette from the oven and transfer them to a cutting board. Let the pizzette stand for 1 minute. Drizzle lightly with extra-virgin olive oil, garnish with the basil, and serve.

MAKES SIXTEEN 2½-INCH PIZZETTE; SERVES 6–8

Pizza with Eggplant, Roasted Peppers & Fontina

Place a pizza stone on a rack in the lower third of the oven and preheat to 450°F. Let the pizza stone heat for 45–60 minutes.

In a bowl, combine the eggplant, onion, ¼ cup olive oil, and the salt. Spread in an even layer on a rimmed baking sheet and place the baking sheet on top of the hot pizza stone in the oven. Roast, turning vegetables over about every 10 minutes, until the eggplant is tender and lightly golden, about 35 minutes.

Meanwhile, place a large sheet of parchment paper on a pizza peel or large rimless baking sheet and place the ball of dough in the center. Coat your fingers with olive oil and press the dough from the center outward into a 12-inch round with a slightly raised edge (see page 15). If the dough springs back, cover it with a clean kitchen towel and let it rest for a few minutes, then continue. Patience is the key here, as the thinner the dough is, the crisper the crust will be. Cover the dough round with a clean kitchen towel and let rise for 15 minutes.

Brush the raised edge of the dough with a light coating of olive oil. Arrange the peppers on the dough, leaving a ½-inch border uncovered. Arrange the eggplant and onion on top of the peppers, and then sprinkle with the oregano and season to taste with pepper. Top with the cheese and capers. Carefully slide the pizza-topped parchment paper from the peel or baking sheet onto the hot pizza stone. Bake until the crust is golden brown and the cheese is bubbling, 9–12 minutes.

Using the pizza peel or rimless baking sheet, remove the pizza from the oven and transfer it to a cutting board. Let stand for 1 minute, and then slice and serve.

MAKES ONE 12-INCH PIZZA; SERVES 2–4

1 small eggplant (about 1 lb), sliced crosswise about ⅜ inch thick

½ large white or yellow onion, thinly sliced

¼ cup olive oil, plus extra for shaping and brushing

1½ tsp coarse salt or kosher salt

1 ball Thin-Crust Pizza Dough (page 20), or Whole-Wheat Pizza Dough (page 25), at room temperature

Marinated Roasted Peppers (page 33)

½ tsp dried oregano

Freshly ground pepper

5 oz Italian fontina cheese, thinly sliced and then torn into bite-sized pieces

1 tbsp capers, rinsed and drained

Tiny capers add big bursts of briny Mediterranean flavor to this pizza. Whether packed in salt or brine, capers should always be rinsed and drained before use.

White Pizza with Garlic & Fresh Herbs

1 ball Thin-Crust Pizza Dough (page 20) or Whole-Wheat Pizza Dough (page 25), at room temperature

Olive oil for shaping and brushing

½ cup whole-milk ricotta cheese

2 cloves garlic, minced

½ cup loosely packed fresh herbs, torn into small pieces

3 oz fresh mozzarella cheese, sliced and torn into bite-sized pieces

2 oz Parmigiano-Reggiano, shaved with a vegetable peeler

Salt and freshly ground pepper

Extra-virgin olive oil for drizzling

Place a pizza stone on a rack in the lower third of the oven and preheat to 450°F. Let the pizza stone heat for 45–60 minutes.

Place a large sheet of parchment paper on a pizza peel or large rimless baking sheet and place the ball of dough in the center. Coat your fingers with olive oil and press the dough from the center outward into a 12-inch round with a slightly raised edge (see page 15). If the dough springs back, cover it with a clean kitchen towel and let it rest for a few minutes, then continue. Patience is the key here, as the thinner the dough is, the crisper the crust will be. Cover the dough round with a clean kitchen towel and let rise for 15 minutes.

Meanwhile, in a bowl, whisk together the ricotta and garlic.

Brush the raised edge of the dough with a light coating of olive oil. Spread the dough evenly with the ricotta mixture, leaving a ½-inch border uncovered. Sprinkle with one-half of the herbs. Top with the mozzarella and Parmigiano-Reggiano and season generously with salt and pepper. Carefully slide the pizza-topped parchment paper from the peel or baking sheet onto the hot pizza stone. Bake until the crust is golden brown and the cheese is bubbling, 9–12 minutes.

Using the pizza peel or rimless baking sheet, remove the pizza from the oven, and transfer it to a cutting board. Let stand for 2 minutes, and then sprinkle the pizza with the remaining herbs and drizzle with extra-virgin olive oil. Slice and serve.

MAKES ONE 12-INCH PIZZA; SERVES 2–4

This pizza is so named because it is made without tomatoes and with only light-colored cheeses. You can use one or any combination of soft, leafy herbs here. Choose from basil, parsley, chervil, tarragon, and oregano. (Use oregano very sparingly.)

Pizza Quattro Formaggi

Place a pizza stone on a rack in the lower third of the oven and preheat to 450°F. Let the pizza stone heat for 45–60 minutes.

Place a large sheet of parchment paper on a pizza peel or large rimless baking sheet and place the ball of dough in the center. Coat your fingers with olive oil and press the dough from the center outward into a 12-inch round with a slightly raised edge (see page 15). If the dough springs back, cover it with a clean kitchen towel and let it rest for a few minutes, then continue. Patience is the key here, as the thinner the dough is, the crisper the crust will be. Cover the dough round with a clean kitchen towel and let rise for 15 minutes.

Brush the raised edge of the dough with a light coating of olive oil. Spread the dough evenly with the tomato sauce, leaving a $1/2$-inch border uncovered. Scatter the basil and arrange the prosciutto, if using, over the sauce. Top with the fresh and smoked mozzarella and the fontina. Season lightly with salt and pepper and sprinkle with the Parmigiano-Reggiano. Carefully slide the pizza-topped parchment onto the hot pizza stone. Bake until the crust is golden brown and the cheese is bubbling, 9–12 minutes.

Using the pizza peel or rimless baking sheet, remove the pizza from the oven and transfer it to a cutting board. Let stand for 1 minute, and then slice and serve.

MAKES ONE 12-INCH PIZZA; SERVES 2–4

Translated from the Italian, this classic pie is called "four cheese pizza." Be sure to use Italian fontina, a lovely smooth-melting cheese, rather than the domestic or Danish variety.

1 ball Thin-Crust Pizza Dough (page 20) or Whole-Wheat Pizza Dough (page 25), at room temperature

Olive oil for shaping and brushing

$1/2$ cup Simple Tomato Sauce (page 26)

$1/3$ cup fresh basil leaves, torn into small pieces

1 thin slice prosciutto, fat removed and torn into small pieces (optional)

2 oz fresh mozzarella cheese, diced or sliced and torn into bite-sized pieces

2 oz smoked mozzarella cheese, shredded

2 oz Italian fontina cheese, shredded

Salt and freshly ground pepper

1 oz Parmigiano-Reggiano, coarsely grated

Pizza with Sun-Dried Tomato Pesto, Arugula & Mozzarella

1 ball Thin-Crust Pizza Dough (page 20) or Whole-Wheat Pizza Dough (page 25), at room temperature

Olive oil for shaping and brushing

1/2 cup Sun-Dried Tomato Pesto (page 29) or Simple Tomato Sauce (page 26)

1 cup baby arugula leaves

1/4 lb fresh mozzarella cheese, sliced and torn into bite-sized pieces

Salt and freshly ground pepper

1 oz Parmigiano-Reggiano, finely grated

3 thin slices prosciutto, torn into small pieces (optional)

Place a pizza stone on a rack in the lower third of the oven and preheat to 450°F. Let the pizza stone heat for 45–60 minutes.

Place a large sheet of parchment paper on a pizza peel or large rimless baking sheet and place the ball of dough in the center. Coat your fingers with olive oil and press the dough from the center outward into a 12-inch round with a slightly raised edge (see page 15). If the dough springs back, cover it with a clean kitchen towel and let it rest for a few minutes, then continue. Patience is the key here, as the thinner the dough is, the crisper the crust will be. Cover the dough round with a clean kitchen towel and let rise for 15 minutes.

Brush the raised edge of the dough with a light coating of olive oil. Spread the dough evenly with the sun-dried tomato pesto, leaving a 1/2-inch border uncovered. Scatter with one-half of the arugula and top with the mozzarella. Season generously with salt and pepper and sprinkle with the Parmigiano-Reggiano. Carefully slide the pizza-topped parchment paper onto the hot pizza stone. Bake until the crust is golden brown and the cheese is bubbling, 9–12 minutes.

Using the pizza peel or rimless baking sheet, remove the pizza from the oven and transfer it to a cutting board. Let stand for 1 minute, then scatter with the remaining arugula leaves and prosciutto, if using. Slice and serve.

MAKES ONE 12-INCH PIZZA; SERVES 2–4

Packed with the one-two punch of the sweet sun-dried tomato pesto and the peppery arugula, this is a bold-flavored pie with modern-day sensibility. Use the optional prosciutto to add another layer of flavor, this one savory and salty.

Mini Pizzas with Herbed Potatoes & Radicchio

Place a pizza stone on a rack in the lower third of the oven and preheat to 450°F. Let the pizza stone heat for 45–60 minutes.

Cut the potatoes into golf ball–sized pieces, if necessary. Place the potatoes in a saucepan, add water to cover by about 2 inches, and season generously with salt. Bring to a boil over high heat, and then reduce the heat and simmer until the potatoes are tender but not mushy, about 10 minutes. Drain and let cool slightly. Slice the potatoes ¼-inch thick. In a bowl, combine the potato slices, 2 teaspoons of the olive oil, the oregano, ¼ teaspoon salt, and pepper to taste. Toss to coat and set aside. Meanwhile, in a frying pan over medium heat, warm the remaining 2 teaspoons olive oil. Add the radicchio and stir frequently until tender and wilted, about 4 minutes. Remove from the heat and stir in the balsamic vinegar.

On a lightly floured work surface, divide the dough into 8 equal balls. Coat your fingers with olive oil and press each ball into a thin, flat 5-inch round. If the dough springs back, cover with a clean kitchen towel and let it rest for a few minutes, then continue. Patience is the key here, as the thinner the rounds are, the crisper the crusts will be. Cover the rounds with a clean kitchen towel and let rise for 10 minutes.

Place a large sheet of parchment paper on a pizza peel or large rimless baking sheet. Space the dough rounds evenly on the parchment paper. Dimple the center of each round with your fingertips, brush with a light coating of olive oil, and season generously with salt and pepper. Spoon the radicchio and arrange the potatoes on each round, dividing evenly, then top with the cheese. Carefully slide the pizza-topped parchment paper from the peel or baking sheet onto the hot pizza stone. Bake until the crusts are golden brown and the cheese is bubbling, 8–10 minutes.

Using the pizza peel or rimless baking sheet, remove the pizzas from the oven and transfer them to a cutting board. Let stand for 1 minute, and then sprinkle with the fresh oregano and serve.

MAKES EIGHT 5-INCH PIZZAS; SERVES 6–8

4 oz small red potatoes

Salt

4 tsp olive oil, plus extra for shaping and brushing

¼ tsp dried oregano

Freshly ground pepper

2 small heads radicchio, quartered, cored, and slivered

2 tsp balsamic vinegar

All-purpose flour for dusting

1 ball Thin-Crust Pizza Dough (page 20) or Whole-Wheat Pizza Dough (page 25), at room temperature

¼ lb low-moisture whole-milk mozzarella cheese, shredded

2 tsp roughly chopped fresh oregano leaves

Pizza with Artichokes, Red Onion & Tapenade

4 baby artichokes, tough
outer leaves removed,
stems trimmed and peeled

Juice of 1 lemon

Salt

2 tbsp olive oil, plus extra
for shaping and brushing

1 small red onion, thinly
sliced and separated
into rings

1 ball Thin-Crust Pizza
Dough (page 20) or
Whole-Wheat Pizza
Dough (page 25), at
room temperature

½ cup Black Olive
Tapenade (page 28)

3 oz fresh goat cheese
or fresh mozzarella, cut
into 1-inch pieces

½ cup Garlicky Bread
Crumbs (see page 59,
optional)

Toss the artichokes with the lemon juice. Fill a saucepan three-fourths full with water, bring to a boil over high heat, and season moderately with salt. Drop in the artichokes and cook until the bases are tender when pierced with a sharp knife, about 7 minutes. Drain and let cool. Cut into quarters and set aside.

In a frying pan over medium heat, warm the 2 tablespoons olive oil. Add the onion and 2 tablespoons water and cook, stirring occasionally, until all the liquid has evaporated, 7–8 minutes. Reduce the heat and cook until the onion is softened and lightly browned, 15–20 minutes.

Place a pizza stone on a rack in the lower third of the oven and preheat to 450°F. Let the pizza stone heat for 45–60 minutes.

Place a large sheet of parchment paper on a pizza peel or large rimless baking sheet and place the ball of dough in the center. Coat your fingers with olive oil and press the dough from the center outward into a 12-inch round with a slightly raised edge (see page 15). If the dough springs back, cover it with a clean kitchen towel and let it rest for a few minutes, then continue. Patience is the key here, as the thinner the dough is, the crisper the crust will be. Cover the dough round with a clean kitchen towel and let rise for 15 minutes.

Brush the raised edge of the dough with a light coating of olive oil. Spread the dough evenly with the tapenade, leaving a ½-inch border uncovered. Spoon the onions and artichokes over the tapenade and top with the cheese. Sprinkle with the bread crumbs, if using. Carefully slide the pizza-topped parchment paper from the peel or baking sheet onto the hot pizza stone. Bake until the crust is golden brown and the cheese is bubbling, 9–12 minutes.

Using the pizza peel or rimless baking sheet, remove the pizza from the oven, and transfer it to a cutting board. Let stand for 1 minute, and then slice and serve.

MAKES ONE 12-INCH PIZZA; SERVES 2–4

Folded Pizza with Asparagus, Olives & Pine Nuts

Place a pizza stone on a rack in the lower third of the oven and preheat to 450°F. Let the pizza stone heat for 45–60 minutes.

Place a large sheet of parchment paper on a pizza peel or large rimless baking sheet and place the ball of dough in the center. Coat your fingers with olive oil and press the dough from the center outward into a 12-inch round with a slightly raised edge (see page 15). If the dough springs back, cover it with a clean kitchen towel and let it rest for a few minutes, then continue. Patience is the key here, as the thinner the dough is, the crisper the crust will be. Cover the dough round with a clean kitchen towel and let rise for 15 minutes.

Meanwhile, on a rimmed baking sheet, toss the asparagus with the 2 teaspoons olive oil and season to taste with salt and pepper. Place the baking sheet on top of the hot pizza stone in the oven and roast the asparagus until golden, 10–12 minutes, turning over with tongs halfway through.

Brush the raised edge and one half of the dough round with a light coating of olive oil. Spread the other half evenly with the ricotta, leaving a ½-inch border uncovered. With a fork, prick the entire surface of the uncovered half. Scatter the olives and pine nuts over the ricotta and top with the asparagus. Season both halves generously with salt and pepper, and top with the Parmigiano-Reggiano. Carefully slide the pizza-topped parchment onto the hot pizza stone. Bake until the crust is golden brown and the cheese is bubbling, 9–12 minutes.

Using the pizza peel or rimless baking sheet, remove the pizza from the oven and transfer it to a cutting board. With a large knife, score the pizza across the middle, between the topped and untopped sides. Fold the untopped half over the topped half to form a half-moon and press down gently. Let the folded pizza stand for 1 minute. Starting from the middle of the folded edge, slice into wedges; drizzle with extra-virgin olive oil, if using, and serve.

MAKES ONE 12-BY-6–INCH FOLDED PIZZA; SERVES 2–3

1 ball Thin-Crust Pizza Dough (page 20) or Whole-Wheat Pizza Dough (page 25), at room temperature

2 tsp olive oil, plus extra for shaping and brushing

½ bunch asparagus (½ lb), tough ends removed and bottom 2 inches of stalks peeled

Salt and freshly ground pepper

⅓ cup whole-milk ricotta cheese

⅓ cup Kalamata olives, pitted and quartered

2 tbsp pine nuts, toasted (see page 31) and roughly chopped

2 oz Parmigiano-Reggiano, shaved with a vegetable peeler

Extra-virgin olive oil for drizzling (optional)

Poultry & Seafood Pizzas

Jerk Chicken Pizza with Smoked Gouda & Red Onion

FOR THE JERK CHICKEN

½ small yellow onion,
thickly sliced

2 green onions, white and
green parts, thickly sliced

1 tsp ground allspice

1 tsp dried thyme

½ tsp ground nutmeg

1 tbsp olive oil

1 habanero chile, stemmed
and seeded

Salt

1 large skinless, boneless
chicken breast half

1 ball Thin-Crust Pizza Dough
(page 20), at room temperature

Olive oil for shaping and
brushing

Salt and freshly ground
pepper

½ small red onion,
thinly sliced

2 tbsp roughly chopped
fresh cilantro leaves, plus
cilantro leaves for garnish

¼ lb smoked Gouda
cheese, shredded

To make the jerk chicken, in a food processor, combine the yellow onion, green onions, allspice, thyme, nutmeg, olive oil, and chile. Season to taste with salt. Process until smooth, about 20 seconds. Transfer the marinade to a baking dish, add the chicken breast, and turn to coat evenly. Cover and refrigerate for 1–4 hours.

Place a pizza stone on a rack in the lower third of the oven and preheat to 450°F. Let the pizza stone heat for 45–60 minutes.

Place a large sheet of parchment paper on a pizza peel or large rimless baking sheet and place the ball of dough in the center. Coat your fingers with olive oil and press the dough from the center outward into a 12-inch round with a slightly raised edge (see page 15). If the dough springs back, cover it with a clean kitchen towel and let it rest for a few minutes, then continue. Patience is the key here, as the thinner the dough is, the crisper the crust will be. Cover the dough round with a clean kitchen towel and let rise for 15 minutes.

Meanwhile, grill, sauté, or broil the marinated chicken breast until well browned, firm, and opaque throughout, about 4 minutes on each side. Transfer to a cutting board and let stand for 5 minutes. Cut the chicken into ¾-inch pieces.

Brush the raised edge of the dough with a light coating of olive oil. Season the dough generously with salt and pepper. Arrange the red onion over the dough, leaving a ½-inch border uncovered. Scatter the chopped cilantro on top and sprinkle with the cheese. Carefully slide the pizza-topped parchment paper from the peel or baking sheet onto the hot pizza stone. Bake until the crust is golden brown and the cheese is bubbling, 9–12 minutes.

Using the pizza peel or rimless baking sheet, remove the pizza from the oven and transfer it to a cutting board. Let stand for 1 minute, and then top with the chicken and cilantro leaves. Slice and serve.

MAKES ONE 12-INCH PIZZA; SERVES 2–4

Pizza with Chicken & Basil Pesto

1 large skinless, boneless chicken breast half or rotisserie chicken breast half, skin removed and shredded

1 tbsp olive oil, plus extra for shaping and brushing

Salt and freshly ground pepper

1 ball Thin-Crust Pizza Dough (page 20) or Whole-Wheat Pizza Dough (page 25), at room temperature

½ cup Basil Pesto (page 31)

2 oz Parmigiano-Reggiano, shaved with a vegetable peeler or coarsely grated

To reduce the pizza preparation time to virtually nothing, use rotisserie chicken and best-quality prepared basil pesto.

If you are using uncooked chicken, pound the chicken breast to an even ⅜-inch thickness, and then brush with the 1 tablespoon olive oil and season to taste with salt and pepper. Grill, sauté, or broil the chicken breast for about 3 minutes on each side until just firm. Transfer to a cutting board and let stand for 5 minutes. Cut the chicken breast crosswise into ⅛-inch slices. Don't worry if the chicken breast is still pink in the center; it will continue cooking in the oven. Set aside. (If you are using rotisserie chicken, you can skip this step.)

Place a pizza stone on a rack in the lower third of the oven and preheat to 450°F. Let the pizza stone heat for 45–60 minutes.

Place a large sheet of parchment paper on a pizza peel or large rimless baking sheet and place the ball of dough in the center. Coat your fingers with olive oil and press the dough from the center outward into a 12-inch round with a slightly raised edge (see page 15). If the dough springs back, cover it with a clean kitchen towel and let it rest for a few minutes, then continue. Patience is the key here, as the thinner the dough is, the crisper the crust will be. Cover the dough round with a clean kitchen towel and let rise for 15 minutes.

Brush the raised edge of the dough with a light coating of olive oil. Season the dough generously with salt and pepper. Spread the dough evenly with the pesto, leaving a ½-inch border uncovered. Arrange the chicken slices over the pesto and top with the Parmigiano-Reggiano. Carefully slide the pizza-topped parchment paper from the peel or baking sheet onto the hot pizza stone. Bake until the crust is golden brown and the cheese is bubbling, 9–12 minutes.

Using the pizza peel or rimless baking sheet, remove the pizza from the oven and transfer it to a cutting board. Let stand for 1 minute, and then slice and serve.

MAKES ONE 12-INCH PIZZA; SERVES 2–4

Pizza with Caramelized Onions & Smoked Duck

Place a pizza stone on a rack in the lower third of the oven and preheat to 450°F. Let the pizza stone heat for 45–60 minutes.

Place a large sheet of parchment paper on a pizza peel or large rimless baking sheet and place the ball of dough in the center. Coat your fingers with olive oil and press the dough from the center outward into a 12-inch round with a slightly raised edge (see page 15). If the dough springs back, cover it with a clean kitchen towel and let it rest for a few minutes, then continue. Patience is the key here, as the thinner the dough is, the crisper the crust will be. Cover the dough round with a clean kitchen towel and let rise for 15 minutes.

Meanwhile, in a small saucepan over medium heat, simmer the balsamic vinegar until syrupy and reduced to 2 tablespoons, 4–8 minutes. Set aside.

Brush the raised edge of the dough with a light coating of olive oil. Spread the caramelized onions evenly over the dough, leaving a ½-inch border uncovered. Arrange the duck breast evenly over the onions and then top with the cheese. Carefully slide the pizza-topped parchment paper from the peel or baking sheet onto the hot pizza stone. Bake until the crust is golden brown and the cheese is bubbling, 9–12 minutes.

Using the pizza peel or rimless baking sheet, remove the pizza from the oven and transfer it to a cutting board. Let stand for 1 minute and drizzle with the balsamic syrup. (If the syrup is too thick to drizzle, re-warm it slightly.) Slice and serve.

MAKES ONE 12-INCH PIZZA; SERVES 2–4

1 ball Thin-Crust Pizza Dough (page 20) or Whole-Wheat Pizza Dough (page 25), at room temperature

Olive oil for shaping and brushing

6 tbsp balsamic vinegar

Savory Caramelized Onions (page 32)

3 oz smoked duck breast, fat and skin removed, then diced

2 oz Manchego or provolone cheese, shaved with a vegetable peeler

This pizza features an interplay of contemporary flavors: the sweetness of the caramelized onions, the smokiness of the duck, and the tartness of the balsamic vinegar. You can substitute smoked turkey—or even smoked ham—for duck breast.

Fresh Clam Pizza with Tomatoes & Bread Crumbs

To make the garlicky bread crumbs, in a food processor with the motor running, add the garlic and process until minced, about 10 seconds. Add the bread, salt, and pepper to taste and process until coarse crumbs form, 5–10 seconds. Add the olive oil and pulse until combined. Measure out ½ cup bread crumbs and set aside. (Extra bread crumbs can be frozen in an airtight container for up to 2 months; thaw for 5 minutes at room temperature before using.)

Place a pizza stone on a rack in the lower third of the oven and preheat to 450°F. Let the pizza stone heat for 45–60 minutes.

Place a large sheet of parchment paper on a pizza peel or large rimless baking sheet and place the ball of dough in the center. Coat your fingers with olive oil and press the dough from the center outward into a 12-inch round with a slightly raised edge (see page 15). If the dough springs back, cover it with a clean kitchen towel and let it rest for a few minutes, then continue. Patience is the key here, as the thinner the dough is, the crisper the crust will be. Cover the dough round with a clean kitchen towel and let rise for 15 minutes. Meanwhile, put the clams and ¼ cup water in a saucepan over medium heat, cover the pan, and cook until the clams open, 5–7 minutes. Discard any that do not open. Remove the clam meat from the shells (you should have about ½ cup) and let dry on a paper towels.

Brush the raised edge of the dough with a light coating of olive oil. Season the dough generously with salt and pepper. Arrange the tomato slices evenly on top, leaving a ½-inch border uncovered. Sprinkle the tomato slices with the oregano, scatter the clams on top, and then sprinkle with the ½ cup of bread crumbs. Carefully slide the pizza-topped parchment paper from the peel or baking sheet onto the hot pizza stone. Bake until the crust is golden brown, 9–12 minutes.

Using the pizza peel or rimless baking sheet, remove the pizza from the oven and transfer it to a cutting board. Garnish with the parsley, slice, and serve.

MAKES ONE 12-INCH PIZZA; SERVES 2–4

FOR THE GARLICKY
BREAD CRUMBS

2 large cloves garlic

5 oz coarse country bread, crusts removed and torn into large pieces

½ tsp salt

Freshly ground pepper

2 tbsp olive oil

1 ball Thin-Crust Pizza Dough (page 20) or Whole-Wheat Pizza Dough (page 25), at room temperature

Olive oil for shaping and brushing

2½ lb littleneck or Manila clams

Salt and freshly ground pepper

1 large plum tomato, thinly sliced

1½ tsp dried oregano

2 tbsp coarsely chopped fresh flat-leaf parsley

Pizza with Shrimp, White Bean Purée & Fresh Herbs

1 ball Thin-Crust Pizza Dough (page 20) or Whole-Wheat Pizza Dough (page 25), at room temperature

2½ tbsp olive oil, plus extra for shaping and brushing

1 cup canned small white beans, rinsed and drained

1 small clove garlic, minced

Salt and freshly ground pepper

½ lb small shrimp, peeled, deveined, and halved lengthwise

¼ tsp dried oregano

2 tbsp Garlicky Bread Crumbs (see page 59; optional)

1 tbsp coarsely chopped fresh basil or flat-leaf parsley

2 tsp finely chopped fresh oregano

Place a pizza stone on a rack in the lower third of the oven and preheat to 450°F. Let the pizza stone heat for 45–60 minutes.

Place a large sheet of parchment paper on a pizza peel or large rimless baking sheet and place the ball of dough in the center. Coat your fingers with olive oil and press the dough from the center outward into a 12-inch round with a slightly raised edge (see page 15). If the dough springs back, cover it with a clean kitchen towel and let it rest for a few minutes, then continue. Patience is the key here, as the thinner the dough is, the crisper the crust will be. Cover the dough round with a clean kitchen towel and let rise for 15 minutes.

Meanwhile, in a food processor, combine the white beans, garlic, ¼ teaspoon salt, pepper to taste, and 1½ tablespoons olive oil. Process until smooth, about 10 seconds. Set aside.

In a bowl, combine the shrimp, dried oregano, ¼ teaspoon salt, pepper to taste, and the remaining 1 tablespoon olive oil.

Brush the raised edge of the dough with a light coating of olive oil. Season the dough generously with salt and pepper. Spread the white bean purée evenly over the dough, leaving a ½-inch border uncovered. Scatter the shrimp and garlicky bread crumbs, if using, over the purée. Carefully slide the pizza-topped parchment paper from the peel or baking sheet onto the hot pizza stone. Bake until the crust is golden brown and the shrimp are pink, about 14 minutes.

Using the pizza peel or rimless baking sheet, remove the pizza from the oven and transfer it to a cutting board. Garnish with the fresh herbs, slice, and serve.

MAKES ONE 12-INCH PIZZA; SERVES 2–4

Pizza with Garlicky Shrimp, Cherry Tomatoes & Parsley

1 ball Thin-Crust Pizza Dough (page 20) or Whole-Wheat Pizza Dough (page 25), at room temperature

1 tbsp olive oil, plus extra for shaping and brushing

½ lb small shrimp, peeled, deveined, and halved lengthwise

2 large cloves garlic, minced

½ tsp dried oregano

Salt and freshly ground pepper

1 cup cherry tomatoes, halved if large, left whole if small

⅓ cup fresh flat-leaf parsley leaves, coarsely chopped

Place a pizza stone on a rack in the lower third of the oven and preheat to 450°F. Let the pizza stone heat for 45–60 minutes.

Place a large sheet of parchment paper on a pizza peel or large rimless baking sheet and place the ball of dough in the center. Coat your fingers with olive oil and press the dough from the center outward into a 12-inch round with a slightly raised edge (see page 15). If the dough springs back, cover it with a clean kitchen towel and let it rest for a few minutes, then continue. Patience is the key here, as the thinner the dough is, the crisper the crust will be. Cover the dough round with a clean kitchen towel and let rise for 15 minutes.

Meanwhile, in a bowl, combine the shrimp, garlic, oregano, and the 1 tablespoon olive oil. Toss to coat the shrimp.

Brush the raised edge of the dough with a light coating of olive oil. Season the dough generously with salt and pepper. Scatter the shrimp and then the cherry tomatoes evenly over the dough, leaving a ½-inch border uncovered. Carefully slide the pizza-topped parchment paper from the peel or baking sheet onto the hot pizza stone. Bake until the crust is golden brown and the shrimp are pink, about 14 minutes.

Using the pizza peel or rimless baking sheet, remove the pizza from the oven and transfer it to a cutting board. Garnish with the parsley, slice, and serve.

MAKES ONE 12-INCH PIZZA; SERVES 2–4

The high heat of the oven is enough to cook these little shrimp, so there is no need to pre-cook them. For the best flavor, choose fresh wild shrimp. Paired with a Caesar salad, this modern pizza makes a light and pleasing summer supper.

Pizza with Wok-Seared Ahi Tuna & Vegetables

Place a pizza stone on a rack in the lower third of the oven and preheat to 450°F. Let the pizza stone heat for 45–60 minutes.

Place a large sheet of parchment paper on a pizza peel or large rimless baking sheet and place the ball of dough in the center. Coat your fingers with peanut oil and press the dough from the center outward into a 12-inch round with a slightly raised edge (see page 15). If the dough springs back, cover it with a clean kitchen towel and let it rest for a few minutes, then continue. Patience is the key here, as the thinner the dough is, the crisper the crust will be. Cover the dough round with a clean kitchen towel and let rise for 15 minutes.

Meanwhile, place a wok or heavy cast-iron frying pan over high heat. When the pan is hot, add the 4 teaspoons peanut oil and swirl to coat the wok. Add the snow peas and asparagus tips and toss until golden and slightly wilted, 1–2 minutes. Using a slotted spoon, transfer the vegetables to a plate. Add the tuna to the wok and cook for 1 minute without stirring. Turn the tuna over with the spoon and cook for 30 seconds more. The tuna will be cooked on the outside, but rare on the inside. Transfer the tuna to the plate with the vegetables and set aside.

Brush the dough with a light coating of peanut oil and season generously with salt and pepper. With a fork, prick the surface of the dough several times, avoiding the raised edge. Sprinkle the dough with 1/2 teaspoon of the sesame seeds. Carefully slide the pizza-topped parchment paper from the peel or baking sheet onto the hot pizza stone. Bake until the crust is golden brown, 8–10 minutes. If any bubbles form, quickly flatten them with the back of a spoon and continue to bake.

Using the pizza peel or rimless baking sheet, remove the pizza from the oven and transfer it to a cutting board. Spread evenly with the hoisin sauce, leaving a 1/2-inch border uncovered. Top with the seared vegetables, tuna, green onions, and the remaining 1/2 teaspoon sesame seeds. Slice and serve.

MAKES ONE 12-INCH PIZZA; SERVES 2–4

1 ball Thin-Crust Pizza Dough (page 20) or Whole-Wheat Pizza Dough (page 25), at room temperature

4 tsp peanut or canola oil, plus extra for shaping and brushing

2 oz snow peas, trimmed and cut crosswise into thirds

18 asparagus tips, cut into 1 1/2-inch lengths

3 oz sashimi-grade Ahi tuna, cut into 1/2-inch cubes

Salt and freshly ground pepper

1 tsp sesame seeds

1/3 cup hoisin sauce

4 green onions, white and light green parts only, thinly sliced

Smoked Salmon Pizzette with Capers & Dill

Place a pizza stone on a rack in the lower third of the oven and preheat to 450°F. Let the pizza stone heat for 45–60 minutes.

On a lightly floured work surface, divide the dough into 16 equal balls. Coat your fingers with olive oil and press each ball into a flat 2½-inch round. If the dough springs back, cover with a clean kitchen towel and let it rest for a few minutes, then continue. Patience is the key here, as the thinner the rounds are, the crisper the crusts will be. Cover the rounds with a kitchen towel and let rise for 10 minutes.

Meanwhile, whisk the 2 tablespoons of dill into the cream cheese and set aside.

Place a large sheet of parchment paper on each of 2 large rimless baking sheets. Space 8 dough rounds evenly on each sheet of parchment paper. Dimple the center the dough rounds with your fingertips, brush the rounds with a light coating of olive oil and season lightly with salt and pepper. With a fork, prick the surface of the dough a few times. Scatter about 2 teaspoons of the onion onto each round and press gently into the dough. Bake the rounds on the baking sheet on the pizza stone, one sheet at a time, for 5 minutes, then, with the back of a spoon, press down the crusts if they are starting to puff up. Continue to bake until the edges of the pizzette are lightly golden, about 5 minutes more.

Remove the pizzette from the oven and transfer them to a cutting board. Let cool 5–10 minutes, then top and serve the pizzette or let them stand for up to 30 minutes, until you are ready to serve: Spread each pizzetta evenly with about 1 tablespoon of the dill–cream cheese mixture, leaving a thin border uncovered. Drape with the smoked salmon, scatter with the capers and the remaining chopped red onion, garnish with dill, and serve.

MAKES SIXTEEN 2½-INCH PIZZETTE; SERVES 6–8

All-purpose flour for dusting

1 ball Thin-Crust Pizza Dough (page 20) or Whole-Wheat Pizza Dough (page 25), at room temperature

Olive oil for shaping and brushing

2 tbsp chopped fresh dill, plus extra for garnish

8 oz whipped cream cheese, at room temperature

Salt and freshly ground pepper

½ red onion, finely chopped

¼ cup capers, rinsed and drained

¼ lb sliced smoked salmon torn into pieces

Meaty Pizzas

Classic Pepperoni Pizza

1 ball Thin-Crust Pizza Dough (page 20) or Whole-Wheat Pizza Dough (page 25), at room temperature

Olive oil for shaping and brushing

¾ cup Simple Tomato Sauce (page 26)

¼ tsp dried oregano

2 oz low-moisture whole-milk mozzarella cheese, shredded

2 oz thinly sliced pepperoni

2 oz pecorino romano or Parmigiano-Reggiano, shaved with a vegetable peeler

Freshly ground pepper

Place a pizza stone on a rack in the lower third of the oven and preheat to 450°F. Let the pizza stone heat for 45–60 minutes.

Place a large sheet of parchment paper on a pizza peel or large rimless baking sheet and place the ball of dough in the center. Coat your fingers with olive oil and press the dough from the center outward into a 12-inch round with a slightly raised edge (see page 15). If the dough springs back, cover it with a clean kitchen towel and let it rest for a few minutes, then continue. Patience is the key here, as the thinner the dough is, the crisper the crust will be. Cover the dough round with a clean kitchen towel and let rise for 15 minutes.

Brush the raised edge of the dough with a light coating of olive oil. Spread the dough evenly with the tomato sauce, leaving a ½-inch border uncovered. Sprinkle the oregano and mozzarella over the sauce, and then top with the pepperoni and pecorino romano. Season to taste with pepper. Carefully slide the pizza-topped parchment paper from the peel or baking sheet onto the hot pizza stone. Bake until the crust is golden brown and the cheese is bubbling, 9–12 minutes.

Using the pizza peel or rimless baking sheet, remove the pizza from the oven and transfer it to a cutting board. Let stand for 2 minutes, and then slice and serve.

MAKES ONE 12-INCH PIZZA; SERVES 2–4

To render some of the fat from the pepperoni (and, incidentally, ensure that it bakes up crisp), cook the slices in a dry frying pan over medium heat for about 5 minutes; drain them briefly on paper towels before topping the pizza.

Pizza with Salami, Fennel & Asiago Cheese

2 tbsp olive oil, plus extra for shaping and brushing

1 small fennel bulb, quartered, cored, and thinly sliced crosswise

Salt

1 ball Thin-Crust Pizza Dough (page 20) or Whole-Wheat Pizza Dough (page 25), at room temperature

¾ cup Simple Tomato Sauce (page 26)

2 oz Genoa-style salami, sliced and torn into bite-sized pieces

2 oz Asiago cheese, sliced and torn into bite-sized pieces

Freshly ground pepper

The wispy, feathery fennel fronds can be chopped and sprinkled onto the finished pizza as a garnish.

Place a pizza stone on a rack in the lower third of the oven and preheat to 450°F. Let the pizza stone heat for 45–60 minutes.

In a frying pan over low heat, warm the 2 tablespoons olive oil. Add the fennel and season lightly with salt. Cover and cook until softened, stirring only occasionally, about 14 minutes. Remove the cover and cook, stirring frequently now, until much of the liquid has evaporated and the fennel is tender and translucent, 5–10 minutes more. Be careful not to let it scorch.

Place a large sheet of parchment paper on a pizza peel or large rimless baking sheet and place the ball of dough in the center. Coat your fingers with olive oil and press the dough from the center outward into a 12-inch round with a slightly raised edge (see page 15). If the dough springs back, cover it with a clean kitchen towel and let it rest for a few minutes, then continue. Patience is the key here, as the thinner the dough is, the crisper the crust will be. Cover the dough round with a clean kitchen towel and let rise for 15 minutes.

Brush the raised edge of the dough with a light coating of olive oil. Spread the dough evenly with the tomato sauce, leaving a ½-inch border uncovered. Scatter the fennel and salami over the sauce, and then top with the Asiago. Season to taste with pepper. Carefully slide the pizza-topped parchment paper from the peel or baking sheet onto the hot pizza stone. Bake until the edges are golden brown and the cheese is bubbling, 9–12 minutes.

Using the pizza peel or rimless baking sheet, remove the pizza from the oven and transfer it to a cutting board. Let stand for 1 minute, and then slice and serve.

MAKES ONE 12-INCH PIZZA; SERVES 2–4

Pizza with Coppa, Soppressata & Prosciutto

Place a pizza stone on a rack in the lower third of the oven and preheat to 450°F. Let the pizza stone heat for 45–60 minutes.

Place a large sheet of parchment paper on a pizza peel or large rimless baking sheet and place the ball of dough in the center. Coat your fingers with olive oil and press the dough from the center outward into a 12-inch round with a slightly raised edge (see page 15). If the dough springs back, cover it with a clean kitchen towel and let it rest for a few minutes, then continue. Patience is the key here, as the thinner the dough is, the crisper the crust will be. Cover the dough round with a clean kitchen towel and let rise for 15 minutes.

Brush the raised edge of the dough with a light coating of olive oil. Spread the dough evenly with the tomato sauce, leaving a ½-inch border uncovered. Layer on the coppa, soppressata, and prosciutto, and then top with the pecorino romano. Season to taste with pepper. Carefully slide the pizza-topped parchment paper from the peel or baking sheet onto the hot pizza stone. Bake until the crust is golden brown, 9–12 minutes.

Using the pizza peel or rimless baking sheet, remove the pizza from the oven and transfer it to a cutting board. Let stand for 1 minute, and then slice and serve.

MAKES ONE 12-INCH PIZZA; SERVES 2–4

This pizza features a savory trio of salumi, or Italian cured meats. You can shuffle the flavors and textures by substituting bresaola (air-dried beef) for the coppa and any other best-quality salami for the soppressata.

1 ball Thin-Crust Pizza Dough (page 20) or Whole-Wheat Pizza Dough (page 25), at room temperature

Olive oil for shaping and brushing

¾ cup Simple Tomato Sauce (page 26)

1 oz coppa, thinly sliced and then torn into bite-sized pieces

1 oz soppressata, thinly sliced and then torn into bite-sized pieces

1 oz prosciutto, thinly sliced and then torn into bite-sized pieces

2 oz pecorino romano or Parmigiano-Reggiano, shaved with a vegetable peeler

Freshly ground pepper

Pizza with Chorizo, Roasted Peppers & Manchego

Place a pizza stone on a rack in the lower third of the oven and preheat to 450°F. Let the pizza stone heat for 45–60 minutes.

Place a large sheet of parchment paper on a pizza peel or large rimless baking sheet and place the ball of dough in the center. Coat your fingers with olive oil and press the dough from the center outward into a 12-inch round with a slightly raised edge (see page 15). If the dough springs back, cover it with a clean kitchen towel and let it rest for a few minutes, then continue. Patience is the key here, as the thinner the dough is, the crisper the crust will be. Cover the dough round with a clean kitchen towel and let rise for 15 minutes.

Brush the raised edge of the dough with a light coating of olive oil. Season the dough lightly with salt and pepper. Arrange the chorizo slices over the dough, leaving a ½-inch border uncovered. Top with the cheese and the roasted peppers. Carefully slide the pizza-topped parchment paper from the peel or baking sheet onto the hot pizza stone. Bake until the edges are golden brown and the cheese is melted, 9–12 minutes.

Using the pizza peel or rimless baking sheet, remove the pizza from the oven and transfer it to a cutting board. Let stand for 1 minute, and then slice and serve.

MAKES ONE 12-INCH PIZZA; SERVES 2–4

1 ball Thin-Crust Pizza Dough (page 20) or Whole-Wheat Pizza Dough (page 25), at room temperature

Olive oil for shaping and brushing

Salt and freshly ground pepper

¼ lb Spanish cured chorizo, thinly sliced

3 oz Manchego cheese, shaved with a vegetable peeler

Marinated Roasted Peppers (page 33)

Manchego is one of the gastronomic prides of Spain and is the most popular of all the Spanish cheeses. If it is unavailable, substitute a young pecorino romano. Be sure to use dry-cured Spanish chorizo on this pizza, not fresh Mexican chorizo.

Pizza with Italian Sausage & Roasted Peppers

1 ball Thin-Crust Pizza Dough (page 20) or Whole-Wheat Pizza Dough (page 25), at room temperature

1 tbsp olive oil, plus extra for shaping and brushing

5 oz sweet Italian sausage, casing removed

Salt and freshly ground pepper

Marinated Roasted Peppers (page 33)

¾ tsp finely chopped fresh oregano leaves

2 oz pecorino romano or Parmigiano-Reggiano, shaved with a vegetable peeler

Place a pizza stone on a rack in the lower third of the oven and preheat to 450°F. Let the pizza stone heat for 45–60 minutes.

Place a large sheet of parchment paper on a pizza peel or large rimless baking sheet and place the ball of dough in the center. Coat your fingers with olive oil and press the dough from the center outward into a 12-inch round with a slightly raised edge (see page 15). If the dough springs back, cover it with a clean kitchen towel and let it rest for a few minutes, then continue. Patience is the key here, as the thinner the dough is, the crisper the crust will be. Cover the dough round with a clean kitchen towel and let rise for 15 minutes.

To cook the sausage, in a cast-iron or nonstick frying pan over medium-low heat, sauté the sausage, breaking it up into small pieces with a wooden spoon, until no trace of pink remains, 5–7 minutes. Drain on paper towels.

Brush the raised edge of the dough with a light coating of olive oil. Season the dough lightly with salt and pepper. Spoon the sausage evenly over the dough, leaving a ½-inch border uncovered. Scatter with the roasted peppers and oregano and top with the pecorino romano. Carefully slide the pizza-topped parchment paper from the peel or baking sheet onto the hot pizza stone. Bake until the crust is golden brown and the cheese is melted, 9–12 minutes.

Using the pizza peel or rimless baking sheet, remove the pizza from the oven and transfer it to a cutting board. Let stand for 1 minute, and then slice and serve.

MAKES ONE 12-INCH PIZZA; SERVES 2–4

If you like spicy flavors, substitute hot Italian sausage for the sweet, sprinkle some red pepper flakes over the pizza, or both. Fresh turkey sausage works well here, too.

Pizza with Prosciutto & Caramelized Onions

Place a pizza stone on a rack in the lower third of the oven and preheat to 450°F. Let the pizza stone heat for 45–60 minutes.

Place a large sheet of parchment paper on a pizza peel or large rimless baking sheet and place the ball of dough in the center. Coat your fingers with olive oil and press the dough from the center outward into a 12-inch round with a slightly raised edge (see page 15). If the dough springs back, cover it with a clean kitchen towel and let it rest for a few minutes, then continue. Patience is the key here, as the thinner the dough is, the crisper the crust will be. Cover the dough round with a clean kitchen towel and let rise for 15 minutes.

Meanwhile, in a dry frying pan over medium heat, cook the prosciutto, stirring occasionally, until crisp, about 5 minutes. Drain on paper towels.

Brush the raised edge of the dough with a light coating of olive oil. Spread the dough evenly with the caramelized onions, leaving a 1/2-inch border uncovered. Scatter the crisped prosciutto over the onions, dot with teaspoonfuls of the mascarpone, and season to taste with pepper. Carefully slide the pizza-topped parchment paper from the peel or baking sheet onto the hot pizza stone. Bake until the crust is golden brown, 9–12 minutes.

Using the pizza peel or rimless baking sheet, remove the pizza from the oven and transfer it to a cutting board. Let stand for 1 minute, and then slice and serve.

MAKES ONE 12-INCH PIZZA; SERVES 2–4

1 ball Thin-Crust Pizza Dough (page 20) or Whole-Wheat Pizza Dough (page 25), at room temperature

2 tbsp olive oil, plus extra for shaping and brushing

3 oz thick-cut prosciutto, diced

Savory Caramelized Onions (page 32)

1/3 cup mascarpone cheese

Freshly ground pepper

When shopping for ingredients for this pizza, ask at the deli counter for a slice of prosciutto about 1/4 inch thick, which you can then cut into perfect dice. Frying the prosciutto before using it as a topping renders some of its fat and crisps its texture.

Quattro Stagione Pizza

1 ball Thin-Crust Pizza
Dough (page 20) or
Whole-Wheat Pizza
Dough (page 25), at
room temperature

1 tbsp olive oil, plus extra
for shaping and brushing

2 oz small cremini
mushrooms, brushed
clean and quartered

Salt

1 clove garlic, minced

$1/2$ cup Simple Tomato
Sauce (page 26)

2 oz low-moisture
whole-milk mozzarella
cheese, shredded

1 oz thinly sliced
prosciutto, torn into
bite-sized pieces

$1/2$ cup marinated artichoke
hearts, well-drained
and slivered

$1/4$ cup Kalamata or Niçoise
olives, pitted and halved

1 oz Parmigiano-Reggiano,
coarsely grated

Freshly ground pepper

Place a pizza stone on a rack in the lower third of the oven and preheat to 450°F. Let the pizza stone heat for 45–60 minutes.

Place a large sheet of parchment paper on a pizza peel or large rimless baking sheet and place the ball of dough in the center. Coat your fingers with olive oil and press the dough from the center outward into a 12-inch round with a slightly raised edge (see page 15). If the dough springs back, cover it with a clean kitchen towel and let it rest for a few minutes, then continue. Patience is the key here, as the thinner the dough is, the crisper the crust will be. Cover the dough round with a clean kitchen towel and let rise for 15 minutes.

Meanwhile, in a frying pan over medium heat, warm the 1 tablespoon olive oil. Add the mushrooms and season lightly with salt. Cook, stirring frequently, until the mushrooms are softened and lightly golden, about 5 minutes. Stir in the garlic and cook for 30 seconds more.

Brush the raised edge of the dough with a light coating of olive oil. Spread the dough evenly with the tomato sauce, leaving a $1/2$-inch border uncovered. Scatter the mozzarella over the tomato sauce. Top one quadrant of dough with the mushrooms, a second with the prosciutto, a third with the artichoke hearts, and the last with the olives. Sprinkle entire pizza with the Parmigiano-Reggiano and season to taste with pepper. Carefully slide the pizza-topped parchment paper from the peel or baking sheet onto the hot pizza stone. Bake until the crust is golden brown and the cheese is bubbling, 9–12 minutes.

Using the pizza peel or rimless baking sheet, remove the pizza from the oven and transfer it to a cutting board. Let stand for 2 minutes, and then slice and serve.

MAKES ONE 12-INCH PIZZA; SERVES 2–4

Quattro stagione, or four seasons, pizza is ideal for serving two. Slice into eighths and serve a wedge of each "season."

Pizza with Potatoes, Pancetta & Taleggio

8 oz small red potatoes

Salt

3 tsp olive oil, plus extra for shaping and brushing

¼ tsp dried oregano

Freshly ground pepper

3 oz pancetta, thickly sliced and then diced

1 ball Thin-Crust Pizza Dough (page 20) or Whole-Wheat Pizza Dough (page 25), at room temperature

¼ lb Taleggio cheese, cut into large cubes

Paired with rich cheese and robust flavors, sliced potatoes are an unusual—but hearty and delicious—topping for pizza.

Place a pizza stone on a rack in the lower third of the oven and preheat to 450°F. Let the pizza stone heat for 45–60 minutes.

Cut the potatoes into golf ball–sized pieces, if necessary. Place the potatoes in a saucepan, add water to cover by about 2 inches, and season generously with salt. Bring to a boil over high heat, and then reduce the heat and simmer until the potatoes are tender but not mushy, about 10 minutes. Drain and let cool slightly. Slice the potatoes ¼-inch thick. In a bowl, combine the potato slices, 2 teaspoons of the olive oil, the oregano, ¼ teaspoon salt, and pepper to taste. Toss to coat and set aside. Meanwhile, in a frying pan over medium-low heat, warm the remaining 1 teaspoon olive oil. Add the pancetta and sauté until crisp, about 4 minutes.

Place a large sheet of parchment paper on a pizza peel or large rimless baking sheet and place the ball of dough in the center. Coat your fingers with olive oil and press the dough from the center outward into a 12-inch round with a slightly raised edge (see page 15). If the dough springs back, cover it with a clean kitchen towel and let it rest for a few minutes, then continue. Patience is the key here, as the thinner the dough is, the crisper the crust will be. Cover the dough round with a clean kitchen towel and let rise for 15 minutes.

Brush the raised edge of the dough with a light coating of olive oil. Season the dough lightly with salt and pepper. Arrange the potato slices on the dough, leaving a ½-inch border uncovered. Scatter the pancetta over the potatoes and top with the cheese. Carefully slide the pizza-topped parchment paper from the peel or baking sheet onto the hot pizza stone. Bake until the edges are golden brown and the cheese is bubbling, 9–12 minutes.

Using the pizza peel or rimless baking sheet, remove the pizza from the oven and transfer it to a cutting board. Let stand for 2 minutes, and then slice and serve.

MAKES ONE 12-INCH PIZZA; SERVES 2–4

Folded Pizza with Roast Beef & Watercress

Place a pizza stone on a rack in the lower third of the oven and preheat to 450°F. Let the pizza stone heat for 45–60 minutes.

Place a large sheet of parchment paper on a pizza peel or large rimless baking sheet and place the ball of dough in the center. Coat your fingers with olive oil and press the dough from the center outward into a 12-inch round with a slightly raised edge (see page 15). If the dough springs back, cover it with a clean kitchen towel and let it rest for a few minutes, then continue. Patience is the key here, as the thinner the dough is, the crisper the crust will be. Cover the dough round with a clean kitchen towel and let rise for 5 minutes.

Brush the dough with a light coating of olive oil and season generously with salt and pepper. With a fork, prick the surface of the dough several times. Carefully slide the pizza-topped parchment paper from the peel or baking sheet onto the hot pizza stone. Bake until golden brown, about 10 minutes.

Meanwhile, in a small bowl, whisk together the sour cream, mayonnaise, horseradish, and dill. Set aside.

Using the pizza peel or rimless baking sheet, remove the pizza from the oven and transfer it to a cutting board. With a large knife, score the pizza across the middle. Let stand for 5 minutes to cool slightly, then spread the pizza evenly with the sour cream mixture, leaving a ¼-inch border uncovered. Arrange the roast beef slices and watercress over one half of the pizza, on one side of the scored line. Fold the pizza in half to form a half-moon and press down gently. Let the folded pizza stand for 3 minutes, pressing down on the crust once or twice. Starting from the middle of the folded edge, slice into wedges and serve.

MAKES ONE 12-BY-6–INCH FOLDED PIZZA; SERVES 2–3

---

1 ball Thin-Crust Pizza Dough (page 20) or Whole-Wheat Pizza Dough (page 25), at room temperature

Olive oil for shaping and brushing

Coarse sea salt

Cracked pepper

⅓ cup sour cream

⅓ cup mayonnaise

2½ tsp prepared horseradish

¾ tsp finely chopped fresh dill

¼ lb rare roast beef, thinly sliced

1 bunch watercress, tough stems removed

This un-Italian spin on the classic roast beef sandwich features a delicious crust and rustic presentation.

Meatball Pizza

To make the meatballs, place the bread in a bowl and cover with ⅓ cup warm water. Let stand for 10 minutes, turning to moisten evenly. Squeeze gently to remove some of the water and then tear the bread into 1-inch chunks. Add the veal, sausage, garlic, parsley, egg white, half of the Parmigiano-Reggiano, ¼ teaspoon salt, and pepper to taste. Mix thoroughly with moistened hands. Form the meat mixture into 10 balls. Place the meatballs on a parchment paper–lined rimmed baking sheet, cover with plastic wrap, and chill for at least 2 hours or up to overnight.

Place a pizza stone on a rack in the lower third of the oven and preheat to 450°F. Let the pizza stone heat for 45–60 minutes.

Place the pan of meatballs directly on the pizza stone and cook until golden brown, about 15 minutes. Let cool and then cut each meatball in half. Meanwhile, in frying pan over medium heat, warm the 1 tablespoon olive oil. Add the onion and season lightly with salt. Sauté until softened, about 8 minutes.

Place a large sheet of parchment paper on a pizza peel or large rimless baking sheet and place the ball of dough in the center. Coat your fingers with olive oil and press the dough from the center outward into a 12-inch round with a slightly raised edge (see page 15). If the dough springs back, cover it with a clean kitchen towel and let it rest for a few minutes, then continue. Patience is the key here, as the thinner the dough is, the crisper the crust will be. Cover the dough round with a clean kitchen towel and let rise for 15 minutes.

Brush the raised edge of the dough with a light coating of olive oil. Spread the dough with the tomato sauce, leaving a ½-inch border uncovered. Scatter the onion over the sauce. Arrange the halved meatballs on top. Sprinkle with the mozzarella and season to taste with pepper. Carefully slide the pizza-topped parchment paper from the peel or baking sheet onto the hot pizza stone. Bake until the crust is golden brown and the cheese is bubbling, 9–12 minutes.

Using the pizza peel or rimless baking sheet, remove the pizza from the oven and transfer it to a cutting board. Let stand for 2 minutes, sprinkle with the remaining Parmigiano-Reggiano, and then slice and serve.

MAKES ONE 12-INCH PIZZA; SERVES 2–4

1 large slice stale white bread, crusts removed

4 oz ground veal or beef, very cold

3 oz sweet or hot Italian sausage, very cold, casing removed

1 small clove garlic, minced

1 tbsp minced fresh flat-leaf parsley

1 large egg white, lightly beaten

2 oz Parmigiano-Reggiano, finely grated

Salt and freshly ground pepper

1 tbsp olive oil, plus extra for shaping and brushing

1 small yellow onion, diced

1 ball Semolina Pizza Dough (page 23), at room temperature

¾ cup Simple Tomato Sauce (page 26)

¼ lb low-moisture whole-milk mozzarella cheese, shredded

Specialty Pizzas

Salad-Topped Grilled Pizzas

All-purpose flour
for dusting

1 ball Thin-Crust Pizza
Dough (page 20) or
Whole-Wheat Pizza
Dough (page 25), at
room temperature

Olive oil for shaping
and brushing

Salt and freshly ground
pepper

3 cloves garlic, thinly sliced

2 small plum tomatoes,
very thinly sliced

2 oz Parmigiano-Reggiano,
shaved with a vegetable
peeler

1 tbsp balsamic vinegar

1 tsp Dijon mustard

2 tbsp extra-virgin olive oil

4 cups loosely packed
mixed spring salad greens

*This fresh-flavored
grilled pizza is the
perfect choice for a
light summer supper
out on the patio.*

Prepare a charcoal or gas grill for indirect-heat grilling (see page 16).

On a lightly floured work surface, divide the dough in half and shape each half into a ball. Cover one of the balls with a clean kitchen towel and set aside. Coat your fingers with olive oil and press the dough outward from the center into a 7-inch round of even thickness. If the dough springs back, cover it with a clean kitchen towel and let it rest for a few minutes, then continue. Patience is the key here, as the thinner the dough is, the crisper the crust will be. Cover the dough round with a clean kitchen towel and let rise for 15 minutes. Meanwhile, shape the second pizza.

Place the first dough round, floured side down, above the oiled, cool part of the grill and close the cover. (No part of the dough should rest directly above the coals or flame during grilling.) Cook until the top of the dough bubbles and the bottom is grill-marked, 3–5 minutes. With a long-handled spatula, flatten the bubbles and then flip the pizza. It is essential to do the following steps quickly, so that you can close the grill as soon as possible: Brush the entire surface of the dough with olive oil and season generously with salt and pepper. Scatter one-half of the garlic over the dough, then arrange one-half of the tomatoes over the top, overlapping as necessary. Top with one-half of the cheese.

Cover the grill and cook the pizza until the edge of the crust is golden and the cheese is melted, 8–10 minutes more. The underside of the pizza should be grill-marked, but not charred. (If cooked too long, the crust will become brittle.) Transfer to a cutting board. Repeat to grill the second dough round.

Meanwhile, in a bowl, whisk together the balsamic vinegar, Dijon mustard, extra-virgin olive oil, and ¼ teaspoon of salt; season to taste with pepper. Add the salad greens and toss with tongs.

Let each pizza cool for 2 minutes, slice it into quarters, top with half of the tossed salad, and serve right away. Or, wait and top both pizzas with the tossed salad and serve them together.

MAKES TWO 7-INCH PIZZAS; SERVES 2

Grilled Pizzas with Zucchini, Roasted Peppers & Pesto

All-purpose flour for dusting

1 ball Thin-Crust Pizza Dough (page 20) or Whole-Wheat Pizza Dough (page 25), at room temperature

1 tbsp olive oil, plus extra for shaping and brushing

2 small zucchini or yellow summer squash, ends trimmed and sliced lengthwise about ³⁄₈-inch thick

Salt and freshly ground pepper

Marinated Roasted Peppers (page 33)

3 oz low-moisture whole-milk mozzarella cheese, cubed

²⁄₃ cup Basil Pesto (page 31)

Prepare a charcoal or gas grill for indirect-heat grilling (see page 16).

On a lightly floured work surface, divide the dough in half and shape each half into a ball. Cover one of the balls with a clean kitchen towel and set aside. Coat your fingers with olive oil and press the dough outward from the center into a 7-inch round of even thickness. If the dough springs back, cover it with a clean kitchen towel and let it rest for a few minutes, then continue. Patience is the key here, as the thinner the dough is, the crisper the crust will be. Cover the dough round with a clean kitchen towel and let rise for 15 minutes. Meanwhile, shape the second pizza.

In a bowl, combine the zucchini and the 1 tablespoon olive oil and season to taste with salt and pepper. Grill over the hot side of the grill until tender and golden, 8–10 minutes, turning once. Cool and cut into ³⁄₄-inch pieces.

Place the first dough round, floured side down, above the oiled, cool part of the grill and close the cover. (No part of the dough should rest directly above the coals or flame during grilling.) Cook until the top of the dough bubbles and the bottom is grill-marked, 3–5 minutes. With a long-handled spatula, flatten the bubbles and then flip the pizza. It is essential to do the following steps quickly, so that you can close the grill as soon as possible: Brush the entire surface of the dough with olive oil and season generously with salt and pepper. Scatter one-half each of the zucchini and roasted peppers over the dough and top with one-half of the cheese.

Cover the grill and cook the pizza until the edge of the crust is golden and the cheese is melted, 8–10 minutes more. The underside of the pizza should be grill-marked, but not charred. (If cooked too long, the crust will become brittle). Transfer to a cutting board. Repeat to grill the second dough round. With a teaspoon, dollop one-half of the pesto evenly over each pizza. Slice and serve the first pizza right away or wait and serve both pizzas together.

MAKES TWO 7-INCH PIZZAS; SERVES 2–4

Olive Oil & Garlic Pizza Breads

Place a pizza stone on a rack in the lower third of the oven and preheat to 475°F. Heat the stone for 45–60 minutes.

In a small bowl, combine the garlic and olive oil. Set aside.

On a lightly floured work surface, divide the dough into 6 equal pieces and shape each into a smooth, round ball. Dust the tops with the flour. With your fingertips, firmly press each ball out into a flat 4- to 5-inch round about ½ inch thick.

Place a large sheet of parchment paper on a pizza peel or large rimless baking sheet. Space the dough rounds evenly on the parchment paper. Brush the rounds generously with one-half of the garlic oil. Carefully slide the dough-topped parchment paper from the peel or baking sheet onto the hot pizza stone. Bake until the loaves are puffed and browned, 7–9 minutes.

Using the pizza peel or rimless baking sheet, remove the loaves from the oven and transfer them to a cutting board or wire rack. Immediately brush the loaves with the remaining garlic oil and sprinkle with the sea salt. Serve the loaves hot, warm, or at room temperature.

MAKES SIX 4-INCH ROUND LOAVES; SERVE 4–6

2 cloves garlic, minced

¼ cup extra-virgin olive oil

All-purpose flour
for dusting

1 ball Thin-Crust Pizza
Dough (page 20), at room
temperature

Fine sea salt for sprinkling

This is a great way to use up any leftover pizza dough. When cooled, these tasty breads can be split and used to make delicious panini. You can also serve them warm alongside your favorite pasta dish for mopping up the sauce.

Pissaladière

In a nonstick frying pan over medium-low heat, warm the oil. Add the onions, 1 tablespoon water, and the thyme. Cover and cook, stirring occasionally, until the onions have softened, about 20 minutes. Uncover and cook, stirring more frequently, until much of the liquid has evaporated and the mixture resembles a thick jam, about 15 minutes more.

Place a pizza stone on a rack in the lower third of the oven and preheat to 450°F. Let the pizza stone heat for 45–60 minutes.

In a bowl, whisk together the egg, 1 tablespoon water, and a pinch of salt.

Line a large baking sheet with parchment paper. Unfold the 2 sheets of puff pastry and space them evenly on the parchment paper. Using a fork, prick the dough all over. Brush both sheets with the egg mixture, being careful not to dribble it over the edges. Spread one-half of the onions evenly over each sheet, leaving a ¼-inch border uncovered. Arrange the anchovies and olives over the onions. Place the baking sheet on the hot pizza stone in the oven. Bake until the edges of the pastry are golden brown, 12–15 minutes.

Garnish each pissaladière with thyme leaves, cut into squares or rectangles, and serve right away, or let cool for up to 30 minutes and serve at room temperature.

MAKES TWO 6-BY-9-INCH PASTRIES; SERVES 6–8

¼ cup olive oil

3 large yellow onions, halved lengthwise and thinly sliced

½ teaspoon fresh thyme leaves, plus extra for garnish

1 large egg

Salt

1 package (2 sheets) frozen puff pastry, thawed

20 anchovy fillets in olive oil, rinsed and patted dry

30 Niçoise or other brine-cured black olives, pitted and halved

Pissaladière is a classic Provençal dish that packs a powerful punch of flavor with layers of onions, olives, and anchovies. Some versions use a yeasted pizza dough–style dough, some a tart pastry. This one is made with tender and flaky puff pastry.

Egg, Sausage & Cheese Breakfast Pizzas

All-purpose flour for dusting

1 ball Semolina Pizza Dough (page 23), at room temperature

Olive oil for shaping and brushing

6 oz sweet or hot Italian sausage, casing removed

4 large eggs, at room temperature

¾ cup Tomato Sauce (page 26; optional)

3 oz low-moisture whole-milk mozzarella cheese, shredded

Salt and freshly ground pepper

1 tbsp chopped fresh chives

A gently cooked egg, savory sausage, and melted cheese on top of warm, hearty pizza dough is a satisfying start to any day.

Place a pizza stone on a rack in the lower third of the oven and preheat to 450°F. Let the pizza stone heat for 45–60 minutes.

On a lightly floured work surface, divide the dough into 4 equal balls. Coat your fingers with olive oil and press each ball of dough into a 5-inch round. Press down on the center of each round to create a well. Cover with a kitchen towel and let rise for 15 minutes.

Meanwhile, in a nonstick frying pan over medium heat, sauté the sausage, breaking it up into small pieces with a wooden spoon, until golden brown, about 6 minutes. Drain on paper towels and set aside. Break each of the eggs into a small ramekin or saucer and set aside.

Line a pizza peel or large rimless baking sheet with parchment paper. Space the dough rounds evenly on the parchment. Dimple the center of each round firmly with your fingertips. Brush each round with a light coating of olive oil and spread evenly with 3 tablespoons tomato sauce, if using, leaving a ¼-inch border uncovered. Arrange the cheese and sausage over the tomato sauce, leaving a space in the center for an egg. Season lightly with salt and pepper. Carefully slide the pizza-topped parchment paper from the peel or baking sheet onto the hot pizza stone. Bake for about 6 minutes. Open the oven door. Without pulling out the oven rack, if possible, use the back of a wooden spoon to press down on the center of each pizza, and then quickly and carefully slide 1 egg onto the center of each pizza. Bake until the egg whites are set and the yolks are still runny, 4–5 minutes more.

Using the pizza peel or rimless baking sheet, remove the pizzas from the oven, and transfer them to a cutting board or wire rack. Let the pizzas stand for 1 minute, sprinkle with the chives, and serve.

MAKES FOUR 5-INCH PIZZAS; SERVES 4

Chicago-Style Spinach & Cheese Deep-Dish Pizza

Place a pizza stone on a rack in the lower third of the oven and preheat to 400°F. Let the pizza stone heat for 45–60 minutes. Brush the bottom and sides of a 10-inch cake pan with olive oil.

On a lightly floured work surface, using a rolling pin, roll out the dough from the center into a flat 14-inch round of even thickness. If the dough springs back, cover it with a clean kitchen towel and let it rest for a few minutes, then continue. Gently fit the dough into the cake pan, pressing it firmly into the corners and up the sides so that there is a 2-inch overhang. Fold the overhanging dough back over itself and crimp to form a thick top edge. With a fork, prick the surface of the dough all over. Cover with a clean kitchen towel and let rise for about 30 minutes.

Bake the dough on the pizza stone until just set, about 4 minutes. (The sides may slip down a little.) Transfer to a wire rack and let cool for 5–10 minutes. In a bowl, combine the mozzarella, ricotta, egg, spinach, ½ teaspoon salt, and pepper to taste. Mix together with a fork until well combined. Scoop the mixture into the warm crust and spread evenly. Spoon the tomato sauce over the top, spread it evenly, and sprinkle with the pecorino romano.

Reduce the oven temperature to 375°F and bake the pizza on the pizza stone for 15 minutes. Rotate the pan 180 degrees and continue to bake until the edge of the crust is dark brown and the cheese is golden, 20–25 minutes more.

Transfer the pan to a wire rack and let the pizza stand for 5 minutes to set. Slice the pizza into wedges and serve directly from the pan or use a spatula to ease the whole pizza onto a cutting board, and then slice into wedges and serve.

MAKES ONE 1-INCH DEEP-DISH PIZZA; SERVES 3–4

Olive oil for brushing

All-purpose flour for dusting

1 ball Deep-Dish Pizza Dough (page 22), at room temperature

3 oz low-moisture whole-milk mozzarella cheese, shredded

¾ cup whole-milk ricotta cheese

1 large egg, lightly beaten

5 oz frozen chopped spinach, thawed and squeezed dry

Salt and freshly ground pepper

1½ cups Simple Tomato Sauce (page 26)

1 oz pecorino romano or Parmigiano-Reggiano, coarsely grated

Saucy, bold, and extra-cheesy deep-dish pizza has many fans—not all of them in Chicago. This is one pizza that is best eaten with a fork and knife.

Sausage & Artichoke Calzone

½ lb sweet or hot Italian sausage, casing removed

1 large egg

1 tbsp milk

All-purpose flour for dusting

1 ball Thin-Crust Pizza Dough (page 20), at room temperature

Salt and freshly ground pepper

1 jar (6½ oz) marinated artichoke hearts, drained and cut into bite-sized pieces

1 oz Parmigiano-Reggiano, finely grated, plus 1 tbsp for sprinkling

2 oz Italian fontina or smoked mozzarella cheese, shredded

6–8 fresh basil leaves, torn into small pieces

½ cup Simple Tomato Sauce (page 26; optional), warmed or at room temperature

Place a pizza stone on a rack in the lower third of the oven and preheat to 450°F. Let the pizza stone heat for 45–60 minutes.

In a frying pan over medium-low heat, sauté the sausage, breaking it up into small pieces with a spoon, until no trace of pink remains, 5–7 minutes. Drain on paper towels and set aside. In a bowl, lightly beat together the egg and milk.

On a lightly floured work surface, divide the dough in half and shape each half into a ball. Place a sheet of parchment paper on the work surface and set the first ball of dough in the center. Cover the second dough ball with a clean kitchen towel and set aside. Dust the top of the dough with flour and, using a rolling pin, roll out to a 7-inch round of even thickness. Repeat with the second ball of dough. Cover both rounds with a clean kitchen towel and let rise for 5 minutes.

Season the first dough round lightly with salt and pepper. Spoon one-half of the artichokes over one half of the dough round, leaving a ¾-inch border uncovered. Top the artichokes with one-half each of the cooked sausage, Parmigiano-Reggiano, fontina, and basil. Make sure the filling isn't mounded too high in the center; it should evenly cover half of the dough round. Gently fold the uncovered half over the covered half to enclose the filling. Firmly pinch and crimp the edges to seal. Repeat with the second dough round. Brush the tops of the calzone with the egg mixture and sprinkle each with ½ tablespoon of the remaining Parmigiano-Reggiano. Cut a small steam vent in the top of each calzone. Using a pizza peel or rimless baking sheet, carefully slide the calzone-topped parchment paper sheets onto the hot pizza stone. Bake until golden, about 15 minutes.

Using the pizza peel or rimless baking sheet, remove the calzone from the oven and transfer to a cutting board. Let stand for 15–20 minutes, then cut into halves and serve warm. If desired, serve the tomato sauce on the side.

MAKES TWO 7-BY-3–INCH CALZONE; SERVES 2–4

Broccoli & Cheese Stromboli

Place a pizza stone on a rack in the lower third of the oven and preheat to 400°F. Let the pizza stone heat for 45–60 minutes.

Fill a saucepan three-fourths full with water, bring to a boil over high heat, and season generously with salt. Drop in the broccoli florets and cook until crisp-tender, 2–3 minutes. Drain and let cool, then coarsely chop. In a bowl, combine the ricotta, provolone, and basil, and mix well.

Place a large sheet of parchment paper on a pizza peel or large rimless baking sheet and place the ball of dough in the center. Dust the top of the dough with flour and, using a rolling pin, roll out to a 9-by-12-inch rectangle of even thickness. If the dough springs back, let it rest, uncovered, for a few minutes, then continue. (It will take persistence to coax the dough into a rectangle.) Cover with a clean kitchen towel and let rise for 10 minutes.

With the long side of the dough facing you, spread the cheese mixture evenly over the dough, leaving a 1-inch border uncovered on all sides. Scatter the broccoli evenly over the cheese and season generously with salt and pepper. Starting with the long edge nearest you, gently roll up the dough, lightly compressing the filling. Crimp firmly to seal, but avoid pressing down too hard. Turn the stuffed roll seam side down, cover with a clean kitchen towel, and let rise for 5 minutes. Brush the roll lightly with olive oil, cut a few small steam vents in the top, and sprinkle with coarse sea salt. Carefully slide the roll-topped parchment onto the hot pizza stone. Bake until golden brown, about 25 minutes.

Using the pizza peel or rimless baking sheet, remove the stromboli from the oven and transfer it to a cutting board. Let the stromboli stand for 15–20 minutes and then use a serrated knife to slice it crosswise into rounds. If desired, serve the tomato sauce on the side.

MAKES ONE 12-INCH STUFFED ROLL; SERVES 4–6

Salt

1½ cups (3 oz) broccoli florets

⅔ cup whole-milk ricotta cheese

2 oz sliced provolone cheese, torn into small pieces

2 tbsp coarsely chopped fresh basil leaves

1 ball Thin-Crust Pizza Dough (page 20), at room temperature

All-purpose flour for dusting

Salt and freshly ground pepper

Olive oil for brushing

Coarse sea salt for sprinkling

1 cup Simple Tomato Sauce (page 26; optional), warmed or at room temperature

Pizza Rustica

1 bunch (¾ lb) Swiss chard

Salt

1 tbsp olive oil, plus extra for shaping and brushing

1 small yellow onion, diced

1¼ cups whole-milk ricotta cheese

3 large eggs

2 tbsp coarsely grated Parmigiano-Reggiano

2 oz provolone or Italian fontina cheese, shredded

10 large fresh basil leaves, torn into small pieces

Freshly ground pepper

1 tbsp milk

2 balls Semolina Pizza Dough (page 23), at room temperature

Marinated Roasted Peppers (page 33)

¼ lb prosciutto, chopped

All-purpose flour for dusting

Place a pizza stone on a rack in the lower third of the oven and preheat to 375°F. Let the pizza stone heat for 45–60 minutes.

Trim the stems from the Swiss chard and discard or reserve for another use. You should have about 4 cups loosely packed leaves. Fill a saucepan three-fourths full with water, bring to a boil over high heat, and season moderately with salt. Cook the chard for 2 minutes. Drain and rinse under cold running water and then squeeze dry, expelling as much excess moisture as possible. Coarsely chop and set aside.

In a frying pan over medium heat, warm the 1 tablespoon olive oil. Add the onion and season lightly with salt. Cook, stirring frequently, until the onion is softened and lightly golden, about 8 minutes. In a bowl, combine the ricotta and 2 of the eggs, and mix well. Stir in the Parmigiano-Reggiano, provolone, basil, ½ teaspoon salt, and pepper to taste. In another bowl, lightly beat together the milk and the remaining egg.

Place a large sheet of parchment paper on the work surface and set one of the balls of dough in the center. Dust the top with flour and, using a rolling pin, roll out to a 12-inch round of even thickness. If the dough springs back, cover it with a clean kitchen towel and let it rest for a few minutes, then continue. Repeat with the second ball of dough, making the size and shape as similar as possible to the first.

With a rubber spatula, spread the ricotta mixture evenly on the first dough round, leaving a 1-inch border uncovered. Top evenly with the chard, onions, roasted peppers, and prosciutto. Lift the second dough round off the parchment paper and center it on top. Firmly pinch and crimp the edges to seal. Brush the surface with the egg-milk mixture and cut 4 or 5 small steam vents in the top. Using a pizza peel or large rimless baking sheet, slide the pizza-topped parchment onto the pizza stone. Bake until the crust is deep golden brown, about 50 minutes.

Using the pizza peel or rimless baking sheet, remove the pizza from the oven and transfer it to a cutting board. Let the pizza stand for 10–15 minutes. Using a serrated knife, slice into wedges and serve.

MAKES ONE 12-INCH DOUBLE-CRUST PIZZA; SERVES 6

Deep-Fried Pizza Dough with Dipping Sauces

All-purpose flour for dusting

1 ball Thin-Crust Pizza Dough (page 20), at room temperature

Vegetable oil for deep frying

1 cup Basil Pesto (page 31) for dipping (optional)

1 cup Sun-Dried Tomato Pesto (page 29) for dipping (optional)

1 cup Simple Tomato Sauce (page 26) for dipping (optional)

On a lightly floured work surface, divide the dough into 16 equal pieces and shape each into a smooth, round ball. Place the dough balls on a large piece of parchment paper, cover with a clean kitchen towel, and let rise for about 10 minutes.

In a deep fryer or large, heavy saucepan over medium-high heat, heat 2–3 inches of vegetable oil until it reaches 375°F on a deep-frying thermometer. Meanwhile, preheat the oven to 200°F. When the oil is hot, carefully add 4 dough balls and fry, using a skimmer to turn frequently, until golden brown all over, about 4 minutes. Using the skimmer, remove the dough balls, drain on a paper towel–lined baking sheet and transfer to the oven. Return the oil to 375°F and fry the next batch of 4 dough balls. Repeat until all the dough balls have been fried.

Serve warm with the desired dipping sauce(s).

MAKES 16 SMALL DOUGH BALLS; SERVES 8–10

Serve these fried dough balls as appetizers with one, two, or even all three sauces for dipping. If you use all three, you will only need about ½ cup of each. It's crucial that you wait for the oil to return to the correct temperature between frying batches; otherwise the dough will absorb too much oil and be unpleasantly greasy.

Mini Pizzas with Pears, Blue Cheese & Honey

Place a pizza stone on a rack in the lower third of the oven and preheat to 450°F. Let the pizza stone heat for 45–60 minutes.

On a lightly floured work surface, divide the dough into 8 equal balls. Coat your fingers with olive oil and press each ball into a thin, flat 5-inch round. If the dough springs back, cover with a clean kitchen towel and let it rest for a few minutes, then continue. Patience is the key here, as the thinner the rounds are, the crisper the crusts will be. Cover with a clean kitchen towel and let rise for 5 minutes.

Place a large sheet of parchment paper on a pizza peel or large rimless baking sheet. Space the dough rounds evenly on the parchment paper. Dimple the center of each round with your fingertips and brush the rounds with the walnut oil.

Arrange the pears on the dough rounds and then scatter with the sage and blue cheese. Season lightly with pepper. Carefully slide the pizza-topped parchment paper from the peel or baking sheet onto the hot pizza stone. Bake until the crust is golden and the cheese is melted, 8–10 minutes.

Using the pizza peel or rimless baking sheet, remove the pizzas from the oven and transfer them to a cutting board or wire rack. Let stand for 1 minute, drizzle lightly with the honey, and serve.

MAKES EIGHT 5-INCH PIZZAS; SERVES 8

All-purpose flour
for dusting

1 ball Thin-Crust Pizza
Dough (page 20) or
Whole-Wheat Pizza
Dough (page 25), at
room temperature

Olive oil for shaping

2 tsp walnut oil

2 small ripe pears, peeled,
cored, and finely diced

6 large fresh sage leaves,
torn into small pieces

½ cup crumbled blue cheese

Freshly ground pepper

2 tbsp honey

A firm, rather than creamy, blue cheese, such as Stilton or Maytag Blue, is best for crumbling. These delicious sweet and savory mini pizzas work equally well as appetizers or as part of a post-dinner cheese course.

Fig Pizza with Mascarpone & Balsamic Syrup

Place a pizza stone on a rack in the lower third of the oven and preheat to 450°F. Let the pizza stone heat for 45–60 minutes.

In a small saucepan over medium heat, simmer the balsamic vinegar until syrupy and reduced to 2 tablespoons, 4–8 minutes. Set aside.

Place a large sheet of parchment paper on a pizza peel or large rimless baking sheet and place the ball of dough in the center. Coat your fingers with olive oil and press the dough from the center outward into a 12-inch round with a slightly raised edge (see page 15). If the dough springs back, cover it with a clean kitchen towel and let it rest for a few minutes, then continue. Patience is the key here, as the thinner the dough is, the crisper the crust will be. Cover with a clean kitchen towel and let rise for 5 minutes.

Brush the dough with the walnut oil. With a fork, prick the surface of the dough several times. Sprinkle the dough evenly with the sugar and nutmeg. Carefully slide the pizza-topped parchment paper from the peel or baking sheet onto the hot pizza stone. Bake until the crust is golden brown, 9–12 minutes. (Watch the pizza as it bakes and, using the back of a spoon, flatten any bubbles that form).

Using the pizza peel or rimless baking sheet, remove the pizza from the oven and transfer it to a cutting board or wire rack. Let the pizza stand until just warm, 10–15 minutes, then spread evenly with the mascarpone, leaving a ½-inch border uncovered. Scatter with the figs and drizzle with the balsamic syrup. (If the syrup is too thick to drizzle, re-warm it slightly). Slice and serve.

MAKES ONE 12-INCH PIZZA; SERVES 4–6

6 tbsp balsamic vinegar

1 ball Thin-Crust Pizza Dough (page 20) or Whole-Wheat Pizza Dough (page 25), at room temperature

Olive oil for shaping

2 teaspoons walnut oil

1 teaspoon sugar

¼ teaspoon ground nutmeg

½ cup mascarpone cheese

6–8 ripe figs, quartered lengthwise

Like a post-modern painting, this stunning pizza will impress with its beauty, and its luscious, summery flavor will delight the taste buds. Serve it as an appetizer or as a light dessert.

To Top it Off

By using the pizza recipes in this book and adding a little creativity of your own, pizza topping possibilities are practically endless. Pick and choose elements from the pizza recipes and combine them with your favorite toppings to create pies that are customized to your own palate. When selecting toppings, try to balance the flavors—for example, counter salty flavors with sweet ones, and spicy flavors with mild ones. It's also a good idea to mix up textures as well as colors and shapes. Shy away from toppings that contain excessive moisture because they will cause the crust to bake up soggy. The chart below contains just a few suggestions to spark your pizza imagination.

Build your pizzas by layering the toppings in they order that they're listed onto the shaped dough that has been brushed with a light coating of olive oil and seasoned to taste with salt and pepper. For oven-baked pies, bake the topped pizzas on a preheated pizza stone in a 450°F oven until the crust is golden brown and the cheese is bubbling, 9–12 minutes.

Spicy Pizza Diavolo with Roasted Peppers & Chicken	Eggplant Parmesan Pizza with Garlicky Bread Crumbs	Pizza with Sun-Dried Tomato Pesto, Sausage & Broccoli Rabe
1 ball Thin-Crust Pizza Dough (page 20), shaped into a 12-inch round	1 ball Semolina Pizza Dough (page 23), shaped into a 12-inch round	1 ball Whole-Wheat Pizza Dough (page 25), shaped into a 12-inch round
½ cup Simple Tomato Sauce (page 26)	1 small eggplant (about 1 lb), roasted (see page 43)	½ cup Sun-Dried Tomato Pesto (page 29)
1 large skinless, boneless chicken breast half, cooked and sliced (see page 56)	½ cup Simple Tomato Sauce (page 26)	5 oz Italian sausage, cooked (see page 74)
Marinated Roasted Peppers (page 33)	2 oz fresh mozzarella cheese, thinly sliced	8 oz broccoli rabe, blanched, drained, and sautéed with garlic
4 oz low-moisture whole-milk mozzarella cheese, shredded	2 oz Parmigiano-Reggiano, coarsely grated	3 oz fresh mozzarella cheese, thinly sliced
¼ cup chopped hot cherry peppers	½ cup Garlicky Bread Crumbs (see page 59)	

Pizza with Pancetta, Wild Mushrooms, Fontina & Thyme

1 ball Whole-Wheat Pizza Dough (page 25), shaped into a 12-inch round

3 oz thickly sliced pancetta, diced and cooked (see page 78)

8 oz mixed wild mushrooms, sautéed with garlic

¼ lb Italian fontina cheese, shredded

1 tsp fresh thyme leaves

Pizza with Caramelized Onions & Gorgonzola Dolcelatte

1 ball Thin-Crust Pizza Dough (page 20), shaped into a 12-inch round

Savory Caramelized Onions (page 32)

½ cup crumbled Gorgonzola dolcelatte cheese

2 tsp chopped fresh sage leaves

Pizza with Pesto, Heirloom Tomatoes & Three Cheeses

1 ball Thin-Crust Pizza Dough (page 20), shaped into a 12-inch round

½ cup Basil Pesto (page 31)

2 heirloom tomatoes, sliced

2 oz fresh mozzarella cheese, thinly sliced

2 oz Asiago cheese, shredded

1 oz Parmigiano-Reggiano, coarsely grated

Southwestern Pizza

1 ball Thin-Crust Pizza Dough (page 20), shaped into a 12-inch round

⅓ cup salsa

4 oz Monterey jack cheese, shredded

5 oz Mexican chorizo, cooked (follow directions for cooking Italian sausage on page 74)

1 green onion, thinly sliced, for garnish

Muffuletta-Inspired Pizza

1 ball Thin-Crust Pizza Dough (page 20), shaped into a 12-inch round

½ cup Black Olive Tapenade (page 28) or chopped green olives

2 oz salami, thinly sliced

2 oz capicola, thinly sliced

2 oz ham, thinly sliced

¼ lb provolone cheese, thinly sliced

Grilled Greek Pizza

Grilled pizza crust (see page 80)

4 cups purchased Greek salad (tomatoes, cucumbers, red onions, green peppers, and olives, with feta cheese, red wine vinegar, and olive oil)

½ teaspoon chopped fresh oregano leaves, for garnish

Glossary

ARUGULA Also known as rocket, this member of the mustard family is a tender leafy green with a slightly bitter, peppery bite. Mature arugula has an assertive bitterness; young, or baby, arugula tends to be mild in flavor and very tender in texture.

BALSAMIC VINEGAR True balsamic vinegar, made from the cooked must of Trebbiano and Lambrusco grapes, comes from Reggio Emilia and Modena in the Emilio-Romagna region of Italy. The longer this sweet-tart vinegar ages, the more viscous and valuable it becomes.

CAPERS The unopened flower buds of a Mediterranean shrub, capers are preserved either by salting or by brining. Their flavor is assertive and pleasantly piquant. Both salted and brined capers should be rinsed and drained well before use.

CHEESE A variety of cheeses are used to top pizzas.

Asiago A cow's-milk cheese from northern Italy, Asiago is a good melting cheese. Young Asiago, sometimes called fresh Asiago, has a semifirm texture and a mild, slightly nutty flavor. Aged Asiago is a hard cheese, similar to Parmesan, and is suitable for grating.

Fontina A rich, semifirm cow's-milk cheese with an earthy, mild flavor, Italian fontina hails from the Piedmont region in northern Italy. Non-Italian versions of the cheese lack the complexity of flavor of Italian fontina, but all types are excellent for melting.

Goat, fresh Also called chèvre, this pure white cheese is made from goat's milk. It has a pleasantly tangy flavor and a texture that ranges from moist, soft, and creamy to dry,

semifirm, and crumbly. It is often sold in logs, but can also be found in small disks, pyramids, and cone shapes.

Manchego From the La Mancha region of Spain, Manchego is a golden-hued, semifirm sheep's-milk cheese dotted with small holes. Its flavor ranges mild to sharp, depending on how long the cheese has been aged.

Mascarpone This thick, rich, and creamy fresh cow's-milk cheese has a mild, buttery flavor with a touch of sweetness and nuttiness. A specialty of Lombardy, Italy, mascarpone is used in both sweet and savory dishes. It is often referred to as Italian cream cheese.

Mozzarella di buffala Sometimes called buffalo mozzarella, this fresh, pure white cheese is made from the milk of water buffalo in the Campania region of Italy. Domestically made versions are also available. It has a delicate, milky flavor with a touch of butteriness, and a stringy texture that is great for melting. Like fresh mozzarella, it is sold packed in water or whey.

Mozzarella, fresh Fresh mozzarella, sometimes called *mozzarella fior di latte*, is a fresh cow's-milk cheese that is white in color and has a slightly springy texture that is good for melting. Its flavor is mild and milky, with hints of sweetness. It is often sold floating in water or whey.

Mozzarella, smoked Smoked mozzarella, sometimes called *mozzarella affumicata*, is fresh mozzarella cheese that has been smoked, which gives it a dark exterior color, a slightly dry, firm texture, and a smoky flavor.

Mozzarella, low-moisture whole-milk In the United States, mozzarella is known as a slightly salty, semisoft cow's-milk cheese with a stringy, elastic texture. It is commonly used as a melting cheese on pizza and in sandwiches. It bears little resemblance to fresh mozzarella made in the Italian tradition, which has a much higher moisture content.

Parmigiano-Reggiano This is true Parmesan cheese made near Parma in northern Italy according to strict standards. Versions made in other countries are also available. No matter its provenance, Parmesan cheese is made from cow's milk and has a nutty flavor and hard, dry texture that is good for grating.

Pecorino romano This Italian cheese made from sheep's milk has a sharp, salty flavor and a hard texture for grating. Many domestically produced pecorino cheeses are made from cow's milk and have less flavor than Italian versions.

Provolone A semifirm Italian cheese made from cow's milk, provolone has a smooth, dense texture. Young provolone is mild and creamy in flavor; aged provolone is drier and boasts a sharper flavor.

Ricotta Traditionally, ricotta is made by recooking the whey that is leftover from the production of other types of cheese. The flavor of ricotta is milky, mild, and slightly sweet, and its texture is very moist and curdy.

Taleggio A very rich, semi-soft, mold-ripened cow's-milk cheese, Taleggio hails from northern Italy. It is molded into 8-inch squares about 2 inches high. Though it is quite aromatic, Taleggio has a buttery and mild flavor.

CHORIZO A coarse pork sausage seasoned with garlic and paprika, Spanish chorizo may be fresh, cured, dried, or smoked, and has a slightly tangy flavor. Do not confuse it with Mexican chorizo, which is a spicy fresh sausage.

COPPA This southern and central Italian cured meat is made from seasoned pork placed into large sausage casings. Its texture is dry and firm, verging on hard. It is cut into very thin slices and served raw.

FENNEL The whitish fennel bulb has a sweet, delicate anise flavor and can be served raw or cooked; the feathery green fronds are often used as a garnish.

FLOUR In addition to all-purpose flour (see page 11), the following flours are used to make pizza doughs.

Bread Milled from the endosperm of hard wheat, bread flour has a higher protein content than all-purpose flour. In pizza and bread baking, it is used to create sturdy, chewy textures with open structures.

Semolina Milled from high-protein durum wheat, semolina has a slightly coarser texture than most wheat flours. Semolina is used in the manufacture of dried pastas and is sometimes called for in pizzas and breads to give them a distinctive hearty, coarse, and rustic texture.

Whole-wheat This flour is milled from whole wheat berries, including the endosperm, bran, and germ, giving the flour its brownish color. Whole-wheat flour lends pizza doughs a slightly dense texture and nutty flavor.

HABANERO CHILES Bright orange, yellow, or green in color, habanero chiles are shaped like tiny lanterns and have a fruity flavor paired with searing heat. Use caution when handling these chiles. Scotch bonnet chiles are a good substitute if habanero chiles are not available.

HOISIN SAUCE This thick brown salty-sweet sauce is used as a condiment in Chinese cuisine, and is often referred to as Chinese barbecue sauce. It is made with soybeans, garlic, vinegar, and chiles and is seasoned with spices.

OLIVES, KALAMATA Salty, brine-cured Kalamata olives are named after the city of Kalamata in southern Greece. These black olives have a dark purple hue; they are large in size with a strong, pungent flavor and a slight fruitiness.

OLIVES, NIÇOISE These small black olives are named for the city of Nice in France's Provence region. Niçoise olives are not very fleshy, but they have a rich, meaty, relatively mellow olive flavor.

PANCETTA Pancetta is unsmoked Italian bacon. It is salted and seasoned with black pepper and other spices before it is rolled into a cylinder and cured. It gives meaty flavor to soups, braises, pasta sauces, and dishes of all kinds.

PESTO An uncooked sauce, pesto is traditionally made with fresh basil, olive oil, pine nuts, cheese, and garlic. Many new takes on pesto have become popular, including versions made with sun-dried tomatoes and other herbs.

PIZZETTE These miniature pizzas are served as appetizers, hors d'oeuvres, or as a part of an antipasto course.

PROSCIUTTO This famed Italian ham is made by lightly seasoning, salt curing, and air drying the hind leg of the pig. The flavor is subtle but intense and slightly sweet.

RADICCHIO A red-leafed chicory, radicchio has a slightly bitter flavor and tender but firm texture. Radicchio di Verona and radicchio di Treviso are the two common varieties; the former is globe shaped and the latter is narrow and tapered, like Belgian endive. Radicchio can be cooked or used raw as a salad green.

SALAMI, GENOA-STYLE This cured Italian sausage is so called because it is made in the tradition of salami of Genoa, Italy. Most often it is made of pork, though beef is sometimes added, and is seasoned with garlic, peppercorns, salt, and red wine.

SOPPRESSATA A specialty of southern Italy, soppressata is a dry-cured salami made from coarsely ground pork. It is seasoned with red pepper and is often pressed during curing, giving the sausage its characteristic slightly flattened shape.

TAPENADE Olives, capers, garlic, anchovies, and olive oil are the assertive flavors in this thick, savory Provençal spread that is used as a dip, condiment, and spread.

TOMATOES, SUN-DRIED Fresh tomatoes dried in the sun (or by other means) take on a deep, intense tomato flavor and chewy, dense texture. They are sold dry-packed in bags or submerged in oil in jars.

TUNA, AHI "Ahi" is the Hawaiian name for yellowfin tuna, which has bright red flesh. When purchasing ahi tuna, ask for "sashimi grade" tuna to ensure you are buying the best-quality fish.

WALNUT OIL Pressed from walnut meats, walnut oil has a rich, nutty flavor and fragrance. It is not used for cooking because much of its flavor is lost when heated; it is often used in salad dressings or for drizzling onto finished dishes just before serving.

WATERCRESS This member of the mustard family has a spicy, peppery bite. The dark-green leaves must be plucked from the fibrous stems and washed well before use. Watercress is often eaten raw as a salad green, but is also used in cooked preparations.

Index

WELDON OWEN
PUBLISHING

814 Montgomery Street, San Francisco, CA 94133
Telephone: 415 291 0100 Fax: 415 291 8841

WELDON OWEN INC.

Chief Executive Officer, Weldon Owen Group John Owen
Chief Executive Officer & President, Weldon Owen Inc. Terry Newell
Chief Financial Officer Simon Fraser
Vice President Sales & New Business Development Amy Kaneko
Vice President and Creative Director Gaye Allen
Vice President and Publisher Hannah Rahill
Executive Editor Jennifer Newens
Senior Editor Dawn Yanagihara
Art Director Kara Church
Senior Designer Ashley Martinez
Production Director Chris Hemesath
Production Manager Michelle Duggan
Color Manager Teri Bell

Photographer David Matheson
Food Stylist Shelly Kaldunski

PIZZA

Conceived and produced by Weldon Owen Inc.

Copyright © 2008 Weldon Owen Inc.

All rights reserved, including the right of reproduction in
whole or in part in any form.

Set in Berthold Akzidenz Grotesk and PMN Caecilia.
Color separations by Embassy Graphics.
Printed and Bound in China by Midas Printing Limited.
First printed in 2008.
10 9 8 7 6 5 4 3 2 1

Library of Congress Cataloging-in-Publication data is available.

ISBN-13: 978-1-7408-9656-6
ISBN-10: 1-7408-9656-4

ACKNOWLEDGMENTS

Weldon Owen wishes to thank the following people for their generous support in producing this book:
Photographer's Assistant Tony Jett; **Food Stylist's Assistant** Lillian Kang; **Copyeditor** Kathryn Shedrick;
Proofreader Kate Washington; **Indexer** Ken DellaPenta; **Photo Consultant** Andrea Stephany